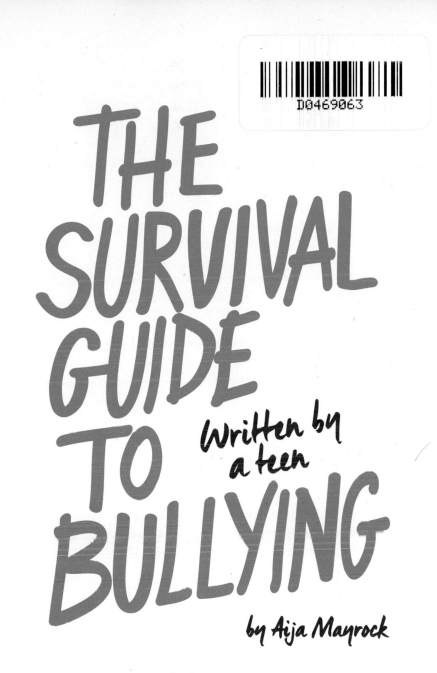

THE SURVIVAL GUIDE TO BULLYING

Written by a teen

by Aija Mayrock

Scholastic Inc.

The Survival Guide to Bullying was vetted by Deborah Temkin, PhD, an expert in the field of bullying, and also by psychotherapist Myrna Fleishman, PhD.

© 2015 Aija Mayrock

ISBN 978-0-545-86053-6

10 9 8 7 6 5 4 3   15 16 17 18 19/0

Printed in the U.S.A.   23
First published July 2015
This edition first printing 2015

Book design by Liz Herzog
Original design © 2014 Omnivore.
Used with permission. All rights reserved.

Stay safe online. Any website addresses and phone numbers listed in the book are correct at the time of going to print. However, website addresses and phone numbers may have changed since that time. Scholastic is not responsible for information or materials that any of the following organizations may share with you or host on their websites. Please be aware that online content can be subject to change and websites and hotlines can contain or offer content that is unsuitable for children. We advise that all children be supervised when using the Internet.

TABLE OF CONTENTS

For the girl and the boy
For the gay and the straight
For the fat and the skinny
For the short and the tall
For the strong and the struggling

You are never alone.

My Gift

BULLYING was the dark cloud over my head. The voices of the kids who bullied me were the raindrops that flooded my day. And their hateful glares were the lightning bolts that I tried my best to dodge.

I didn't realize how much bullying had taken over my life until my family and I moved across the country at the end of 8th grade.

I realized how much I had been suffering, but I also realized how strong I was. I started writing poems, screenplays, and stories. I put all of my pain into my work. I had finally found this incredible outlet. And through this outlet, I found my first mission in life.

I knew that there were millions of kids all over the world suffering in silence from bullying. In my sleep, I could feel their fear, their helplessness, and their pain. I dreamed of a way that I could help them and show them that they weren't alone in their battle.

One day, I realized that I had to create a little yet powerful survival guide that any kid could use when he or she was being bullied in the gym, the cafeteria, the locker room, the classroom, the hallways—anywhere. A guide that could help any kid dry their tears and put a smile on their face. A guide that could convince a kid to come out of that bathroom stall that they had locked themselves into and see the flickering light at the end of the tunnel. A guide that could be a road map, a flashlight, or a friend.

So here it is. This book is my gift to you. The advice is based on all of my experiences throughout the many years I was bullied and conversations with parents, teachers, and other victims of bullying. I also collaborated with mental health professionals.

Welcome to my book and your new beginning!

My Story

Eight years old I arrived
In front of this cluster of stone buildings
Ready to thrive
Feeling so alive
Not knowing that this place would be my
    fight to survive

At nine I tried to be myself
To dress to impress only myself
To write to feel alive
But I was beaten down
For just trying to be me

At ten I tried to fit in
Knowing that it had been hell
I felt like I was trapped in a cell
So I dressed the same
To fit into their game
But my soul had a name
And it wasn't the same
As the other players in the game

3

ELEVEN

At eleven
I kept quiet
I couldn't take my internal riot
I needed an escape
But I was trapped in this game
Of words and pain
And my writing had taken flight
It even got away from the game
But I had to stay
It wasn't my turn to run away

Twelve

At twelve
I craved friends and fame
I dreamed of being in movies
Where you could escape
Shift shape
Into different lives
And never need to arrive back into your
   first life
But I was told I would never be
Anything more than debris
I was bullied for my desire to act
And retreated out to sea
But I was holding a pirate key
In dreams or in reality
I needed one thing to hold on to
And that was me

At thirteen I was feeling the darkness
    creep into my dreams
I was scared of losing myself
In their hateful glares
And disgusting comments
About my beauty and body
Soon food started to taste like their stares
And I would walk around
Looking down at myself
Running from the darkness
Creeping
Behind . . .

At fourteen my day had come
To run away
And it truly was
A freeing day
I ran to the place where movies were made
Hoping it would be a Band-Aid

At fifteen I felt free as can be
From my bullies
But on Halloween
A monster cyberstalked
And bullied me
I knew I couldn't flee
And at this moment

My writing saved me
I wrote of bullies and suicide
It doesn't mean that I wanted to die
But I wanted the message to be said
I stayed with my pain
Didn't run from it
And so I won from it
But all of the darkness of my past didn't
    leave with words and awards
And food looked dark and tasted
    like cardboard
When I looked in the mirror
My body was covered in the words my
    bullies had said
"Fat" "Disgusting" "Nauseating"
Filled my ears and eyes
Until nothing could make me smile

At sixteen
I cried as kids killed themselves
Night after night
To escape their darkness
Take flight, out of this life
And I couldn't sleep at night
Knowing that I wasn't teaching them how
    to fight

So I started to write this book
To show you that there is a secret hook
   to surviving this moment in time

At seventeen
I feel like I have tamed the voices
The images
I know my name
And my path in this game
But in order to end this book
I must take one last look
At the school where endless pain
   took reign

And I am sitting here
Outside the empty middle school
Where all of this ruled
Looking in to the hallway
And for a second I see
A little eleven-year-old girl facing me
She is wearing a skirt and collared shirt
She is so beautiful
So sweet
And then I realize
That it's me . . .

She waves at me
And smiles   *beautiful*
She lets one tear escape her eyes
And I let one leave mine
She looks at me for a second more
Then disappears through some
   invisible door

✱ INTRODUCTION ✱

Congratulations!

You have made it this far. You have bought or been given this book. You have acknowledged that you're being bullied and you want things to change. This is an important step. To do this, you need to get to know the Real You. This is not about changing. Instead, it's about finding and embracing who you really are. The Real You is not far away. In fact, it's been deep inside you all along. I hope that this book will help you discover who that beautiful person is.

I know what it's like to be hated for no reason, to be isolated with no explanation, and to feel alone with no end in sight. So in this book, I will try to help you deal with bullying every step of the way. I will tell you how I got through my tough times. And I'll tell you some of my story. But I will not dwell too much on what knocked me down, because what knocked me down is not as important as what made me stand up.

I'm not a doctor, teacher, or therapist. I'm just a girl. But I'm a girl who has not only survived bullying—I have thrived because of it.

I went through very difficult times, but that showed me just how strong I was. It also made me want to use my voice to help others, to talk about important issues, and to make a change in this world. And that is why I wrote this book.

I want you and every other kid who is suffering to be able to come out the other end. And I want you to have an incredible life.

* I want you to be happy.
* I want you to achieve your wildest dreams.
* I want you to be able to let go of your past.

I can't tell you that the methods in this book will work for you, but I can promise you possibilities. So take what you can from this book and create your own journey. The bullying is what's here and now, but it doesn't exist in your future.

You are stronger than you know. You will survive. You will thrive.

Creating your new life won't be as difficult as you think. You are on your way toward a happier future.

The Old You and the Real You

I will be here with you as you begin the journey of letting go of the Old You and discovering the Real You. It isn't easy to leave bullying in the past when being bullied is such a part of your present.

When you're bullied, you become used to being alone and disliked. You will see that you have to let go of your pain and your past to become the Real You and start a new phase of your life.

Don't Count on a Superhero

I have learned that no one is waiting around the corner to save me or you. There won't be a superhero who flies through your window and whisks you off to a perfect world. You have to realize that bullying is not your fault, but it is your problem. Knowing this is the first step to dealing with bullying.

I learned that, in order to survive, I had to become the hero in my own life. I had to save myself. You must do the same.

The Roems

I created the term "roem." It is a rap poem. I wrote one to introduce every chapter. The first one is my story. I wrote these roems as I went through the process of healing from bullying from ages 16 to 18. They are inspired by the rhythm and beat of rap music, which was incredibly important to me throughout my most difficult years. I found rap to be strengthening and inspirational, so I wanted to create my own form of it. I hope they help you, too. I hope you can relate to them and that they calm you in your most difficult moments. Feel free to write your own. Tell your story. It really helps, I promise.

Here Is Your Road Map

Each step moves you toward your new beginning and discovering the Real You.

CHAPTER ONE

Why Me: Because You're a Normal Kid

You are normal, special, and unique. But it doesn't always feel this way when you're bullied.

CHAPTER TWO

The Old You: Stuck in an Act

You need to accept yourself for who you are. Don't try to be someone you're not. Once you learn to embrace the Real You, your life will get better.

CHAPTER THREE

The Real You: Out with the Old, In with the New

Become who you want to be. Love yourself. Dream about what you want to create in your life. Your future will be brighter and the bullying will seem distant.

CHAPTER FOUR

Getting Help: Becoming Your Own Superhero

Don't be afraid to ask for help from your parents and teachers. I know it's scary, but you shouldn't go through this alone. Step up and become your own superhero.

CHAPTER FIVE

Fear: The Dark Tunnel

We all have fears. You are not alone. Embrace your fears and it will help you find the light at the end of the tunnel.

CHAPTER SIX

Battlefield Scenarios: Surviving in the Trenches

Prepare and plan for all scenarios in and out of school. You must always be safe. You are your number one priority. Be one step ahead of everyone else.

CHAPTER SEVEN

#Cyberbullying: Pressing Delete

The Internet is a world of the unknown. You need to know how to protect yourself.

CHAPTER EIGHT

Creativity: Being Happy Again

Believe in yourself and your potential. Express yourself through whatever you enjoy. You are an endless possibility.

CHAPTER NINE

Benefits of Being Bullied: Finding the Light at the End of the Tunnel

There are actually many benefits of being bullied—you just have to be willing to see them.

WHAT IS BULLYING?

Before we take the first step together, let's look at what bullying is.

According to Stopbullying.gov:

- Bullying is unwanted, aggressive behavior.
- This behavior is based on there being a difference in power. This difference can come from physical strength, access to embarrassing information, or popularity.
- The behavior has to happen more than once and have the possibility of continuing.
- Threats, rumors, attacking someone physically or verbally, and excluding someone from a group on purpose are examples of bullying.

THERE ARE THREE TYPES OF BULLYING:

Verbal bullying

- Teasing
- Name-calling
- Putting someone down
- Threatening to cause harm
- Saying inappropriate sexual comments

Social bullying

- Leaving someone out on purpose
- Telling other kids not to be friends with someone
- Spreading rumors about someone
- Embarrassing someone in public

Physical bullying

- Hitting/kicking/pinching
- Spitting
- Tripping/pushing
- Taking or breaking someone's things
- Making mean or rude hand gestures

YOU MAY ALSO WONDER WHY KIDS BULLY

Here's some info according to Stopbullying.gov:

* They might be bullied at home by their parents, siblings, neighbors, etc.
* They might be very self-conscious, so they take it out on others.
* They might not realize that they are bullies.
* They might believe that behaving this way is "normal."
* They might gain popularity and feel more powerful by putting others down.

The Circle of Bullying

There are many roles that kids can play in a bullying situation. Kids can bully others, they can be bullied, or they may observe bullying.

WHEN A KID SEES BULLYING, HE OR SHE MAY:

* **Assist** in the bullying. While some kids do not start or lead the bullying, they may occasionally join in. This can encourage the bullying to continue.

* **Reinforce** the bullying by watching and laughing. This can also encourage the bullying to continue.

* Be an **outsider** and watch and do nothing.

* Be a **defender** by taking a stand and trying to stop the bullying.

No matter where a kid is in the circle of bullying, he or she needs support and guidance and should ask for help from a parent or teacher.

Glass Rain

You can't even explain the pain
As if you were caught in glass rain
The way they stare at you
The things they say to you

Makes you feel like your purpose
Is worthless
You're just part of their game

And it drives you insane
To think that those names
Must have come from some
Grain
Of truth
It's like a sharp tooth
Digging in to your flesh
The blood clears
Into tears
And you find yourself alone
At school or at home
With just the company of your fears
Your tears may have cleared
But the pain remains
You'll do anything to contain it

And just as it begins to leave
Faces flood you
Voices condone
You are no longer alone

Your mind takes over
It's playing red rover
With you
Making you a recluse
Within your own mind
Running wild inside
Your soul
And they become a big role
In your inner life
But never forget . . .
You have strife
And the power to create
A new life

Your MIND
Your SOUL

LIFe

CHAPTER 1

Why Me?

Because You're a Normal Kid

One day in 3rd grade, a girl came to visit our school. She was planning to attend the following year. Let's call her Ally. Immediately, it seemed like everyone was so excited for her to come to school next year. I was new at the school that year, too, and I couldn't figure out why no one was excited when I came. I couldn't figure out why no one would sit with me at lunch or even answer me when I said hi. So I decided to ask a girl in my class one day. Let's call her Rebecca.

"Why is everyone so excited for Ally to come to school?" I asked.

"Because she's so pretty and skinny and perfect," Rebecca said.

"Why wasn't anyone excited when I came to this school?" I asked.

"Because you're not like her," Rebecca responded.

I was just eight years old and didn't understand. All I wanted to do was come to school to play on the playground and hang out with my classmates. I wasn't thinking about being "perfect."

It took me so many years to realize Rebecca was right. No one was excited for me to come to school because I didn't fit the "pretty, skinny, and perfect" mold like Ally did. I was perfect in my own way, but the other kids didn't see that. And, in part, that is why I wasn't accepted.

"Why ME?" I would always ask myself.

I will never know for sure why I was bullied. All I know for sure is they chose me. I was the girl they decided to be mean to. And one day, a few years later, I asked Rebecca why everyone was still so mean to me. She said: "It's not personal; it's just you."

How can something be about me but not be personal? I realized that it made perfect sense. It really wasn't personal. The bullying may have started with something someone didn't like about me, but it continued because I was the one that they decided to bully. It wasn't about me anymore. It was me or someone else, and they went with me.

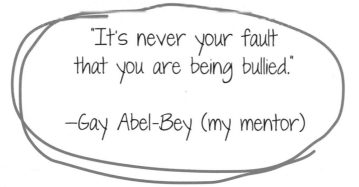

"It's never your fault that you are being bullied."

—Gay Abel-Bey (my mentor)

We want to believe that there is something about us that is a target, something we can change. Is it my voice? My skin? My body? My walk? My hair color? My clothing? But it isn't. You are perfect in your own way. It's not you that has the problem, it's the bullies. I promise.

Even if you struggle with your speech, weight, or skin, that doesn't make YOU the problem. No one is perfect. So if you are bullied because you're a little different, it's really the bullies who have a problem.

For years I wondered what was so wrong with me that I had to be bullied relentlessly. To be perfectly honest with you, there are still some days when I still wonder WHY? What did people hate so much about me that made them want to be brutal toward me? What could I have changed about myself? I will never have an answer to that, except that I am who I am. And finally, after years of hating and hiding who I am:

I love what makes me unique.

THINGS KIDS HAVE BEEN BULLIED ABOUT:

Looks skinny/fat
Looks old/young/weird
Gets sick a lot
Is disabled
Gets good grades/bad grades
Where he lives
Clothes she wears
Color of skin
Country he's from
Religion she observes
His parents/brother/sister
Family is poor/rich
Someone in family has disabilities
Too tall/too short
She's in special education
He gets angry a lot
Can't get along with others
She's gay
He's trans
Way he walks
Jealousy
No reason at all

You're Just a Regular Kid. Believe It, It's True!

There is nothing wrong with the things on this list of reasons. There probably isn't a person in the world who wouldn't fall into eight or nine of these categories. So you're a short student who looks young, has good grades, comes from a poor family, and goes to church. You also happen to have a brother or sister in special education, and yes, your skin has a color. I just listed seven reasons and they all seem perfectly normal to me.

So let's ask the questions again: **Why me? Why you?**

There is absolutely nothing bizarre or weird on this list. Everybody is on this list. You're just you, plain and simple you. You're being bullied because you're normal and healthy.

SURVIVAL TIP

Repeat this three times a day.

There is
NOTHING WRONG
with me.

Below are a few things that make me ME. I used to get bullied for these things, but now I love them about myself. They are part of what makes me unique and special.

I'm quiet. I was quiet because I was always watching and observing everyone else. I love this about myself now. Sometimes when you sit back and listen, you can learn a lot about everyone around you.

I'm creative. Maybe some people noticed this when I was in school and they felt it made me different. But now I know that this is who I am. It's what allowed me to write this book. I couldn't be happier to be creative. It just took a while to accept it.

I'm polite. I'm a believer in respect for others. But some of the kids I went to school with thought this was weird or that I was being a teacher's pet. But being polite has led me to meeting and gaining the respect of people who are important to me. I wouldn't change this for the world.

I have long, thick hair. I used to hate my hair because the kids who bullied me said it was disgusting. I wanted to chop it all off. But now I feel that my hair is one of my best features—I've even been asked to be a hair model!

What makes you YOU? Write your own list! You never know—what makes you different today might play a big part in who you will become in the future. You may even come to love these parts of yourself like I did.

Think about it: You may still believe that there is something wrong with you and that is why you are being bullied. When I found out how many of the successful people I look up to had been bullied, it completely changed my perspective on the situation. I no longer felt alone. I realized that no matter how beautiful, smart, successful, talented, or famous a person is, he or she can still have been bullied. Look it up online and read about all of the celebrities who have suffered just like you and me. Read about how they overcame bullying. You just might be inspired by their stories.

Right now there are thousands of kids
being bullied all over the world. And so many of
these kids will become someone great one day.
So many of these kids are destined to be
doctors, actors, scientists, writers,
politicians, musicians, anything!
The path seems painful and difficult now.
But the difficulty WILL NOT last forever.
Do not give up.
You are destined for something.

Vitality

SPACE

Have you ever stared into space
And dreamt of a place
Where you could escape
The endless chase
Of their faces
Their words
It makes you feel like seeking the land of
    no return
Because the pain is so great
It makes it seem like it's too late
For happiness
But happiness
Cannot be stolen
It can be bruised and diffused
Lost and forgot
But it's never too late
To regain it
Then take it on a trip
To a land where you are free
From all misery
Where you can believe in yourself
Where you can love yourself
And leave in one piece

BRUISED

As a being
That deserves that same
Cease fire
As a being that deserves
To be admired
To be inspired
By life
As a being who has rights
And wants to fight
For a life that seems so hard
But I promise you it's not all barred
    windows and doors
There's a place for you and more . . .
Where you can be free
Of your pain
Submerged in your fantasy
Far from reality
But don't you see
The brutality
Will soon meet
Its lethality
And you will once again discover
Vitality

fight

See

✱ CHAPTER TWO ✱

The Old You:
Stuck in an Act

Before I was bullied, I was totally my own person. I dressed tomboyish and wasn't obsessed with what I looked like. I laughed and smiled whenever I wanted. I loved music, books, and movies that weren't necessarily "cool." I was proud of being unique and loved myself. Then I started getting bullied for the way I dressed, my weight, my appearance, my voice, my laugh—literally everything about myself that I was happy with. I felt like there must be something really wrong with me. All I wanted to do was fit in. So I figured that if I were like the people who bullied me, then maybe things would get better. So I changed how I dressed, the music I listened to, and the way I walked and talked. I thought this would work. But guess what? It didn't.

Then when my family moved to California I tried doing the same thing to fit in. And guess what? It actually worked for one year. And I was happy. Well, sort of.

You can't really be happy if you are pretending to be someone you're not. In a way, you're bullying yourself.

You're telling yourself that you aren't good enough or special enough, so you have to be someone else. You are lowering your self-esteem and making the situation worse. I know because I lived this way. **After one year of pretending to be someone I was not, I gave up on pretending.** That's when I started to get into writing. And to be honest, I was completely ostracized because of it. At the time, no one wanted to hang out with me because writing was not something anyone thought was cool.

I discovered what I loved and as a result I was isolated from all of my peers. I guess that's what people mean when they say, "You have to make sacrifices in life."

I made that sacrifice. I stopped trying to be friends with people who weren't interested in me. And that meant I spent my first two years of high school completely alone. It's really hard to imagine having friends when you spend so much time by yourself. But I can promise you that it's possible.

I found one friend in 10th grade. We weren't very close and our friendship didn't last long, but it was still nice to have someone to be with at school. She didn't have friends either and it was a relief to be there for each other.

Some friends are meant to be in your life for a short time, while others stay in your life forever. I met my first good friends in 11th grade. I think that I really connected with these people because I met them at an acting camp where we all shared the same passion. I'm still friends with these kids today.

I can promise you that although it takes time and effort, you will be happy and have a better life one day. You will not always be bullied and you will find friends who accept you for who you are.

The Old You is who you may be pretending to be, because you want to be liked by your peers. The Old You is filled with the things you do to impress people. It's the part of you that will do anything to be liked, despite your beliefs—you're stuck in an act. And I understand that part of you. For so many years, I lived like this because all I wanted was to be accepted. But when I discovered the true me, my life was transformed. I finally felt free to do the things I wanted to do, despite what others thought of me. So I am going to help you make your transition from the Old You to the Real You.

Here are three quizzes to help you understand how you're feeling. You need to check in with yourself and understand how you are living your life right now. If you are not being the Real You, then you might be feeling unhappy. That's okay. We've all felt this way at one point or another. But if you don't do anything to help yourself, your life won't get any better. The lists and tips that I have created for you can help you start to turn your life around!

WHAT'S GOING ON IN GENERAL?

Do you cry often?

Yes / No / Maybe

Do you have trouble breathing?

Yes / No / Maybe

Do you get headaches?

Yes / No / Maybe

Do you get stomachaches?

Yes / No / Maybe

Do you feel like you are jumping out of your skin?

Yes / No / Maybe

If you answered mainly "Yes" and "Maybe," you're not doing very well. I've been there, too. I've felt all of these things at different points during the time I was bullied. I encourage you to talk to someone you trust—a family member, friend, or teacher. Tell this person honestly how you feel and ask what you should do.

I would also recommend checking out **Chapter 3: The Real You, Chapter 4: Getting Help,** and **Chapter 8: Creativity**. I think the tips in those chapters will help you feel better.

WHAT ABOUT SCHOOL?

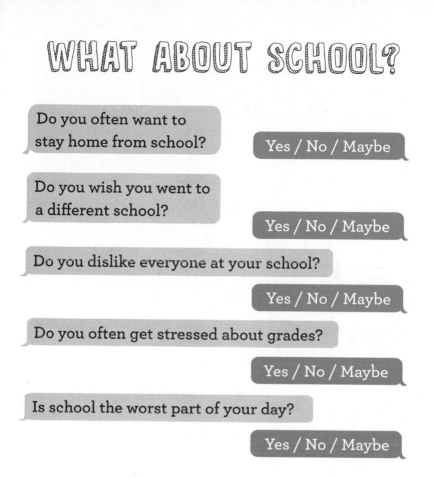

Do you often want to
stay home from school?

Yes / No / Maybe

Do you wish you went to
a different school?

Yes / No / Maybe

Do you dislike everyone at your school?

Yes / No / Maybe

Do you often get stressed about grades?

Yes / No / Maybe

Is school the worst part of your day?

Yes / No / Maybe

If you answered "Yes" or "Maybe" to most of these questions, you are obviously very unhappy at your school. I've been there, too. I spent five years at a school in New York that I was miserable at. When my family and I moved to California, I had one great year at my new school. But the next two years were really hard. I wasn't getting bullied, but I wasn't included socially at all. I was alone most of the time.

I was very fortunate to be able to change schools for 11th and 12th grade. I was incredibly happy and had so many friends at my new school. Not every class or school is one size fits all. And that's okay. There isn't anything wrong with you. Once again, I encourage you to talk to someone you really trust and see if there are options for making things better at the school you are at.

For lots of advice that helped me through my school days, check out the Six Stepping Stones in **Chapter 3: The Real You**, as well as the tips in **Chapter 4: Getting Help** and **Chapter 6: Battlefield Scenarios**.

WHAT ABOUT ONLINE?

Do you check Facebook, Instagram, Twitter, etc., often to see if you got likes?

Yes / No / Maybe

Do you get upset if you don't get likes?

Yes / No / Maybe

Do you get upset when people unfollow you on social media?

Yes / No / Maybe

Do you feel like you need to prove yourself on social media?

Yes / No / Maybe

Do you feel like you have to act out to be liked?

Yes / No / Maybe

If you answered mainly "Yes" or "Maybe," social media is impacting your life to an extent that is hurting your confidence and happiness. You need to control how it makes you feel.

When I was in 9th grade, Facebook became so negative for me because people were harassing me on it. No matter how many times I blocked these people, they continued to find ways to harass me. So I made my account as private as possible and I stopped going on Facebook as much. The separation helped me feel better and gave me time to focus on things that were important in my life.

I suggest you read **Chapter 7: #Cyberbullying** for more tips and ideas to help you out with your online life.

SURVIVAL TIP

Remember that what you're going through is not easy.

Find someone you trust and feel good around. Tell him or her what is going on with you and see what advice is offered. After that, treat yourself to something you love, like your favorite food or TV show, or take a walk in the park. It's all going to be okay!

Check out this game. Even when everything feels bad, you still have the power to turn things around for yourself. Pick out the first three words you see and make them the theme of your day. I do this all the time to set the tone for my day. For instance, I want there to be LOVE, FREEDOM, and EXCITEMENT in my day. So I'm going to make that happen. You can do it, too.

```
F  R  E  E  D  O  M  C  L  Y
D  U  Z  V  Q  J  T  O  H  C
U  X  N  Q  T  V  Y  N  A  X
H  I  I  X  I  Z  L  F  P  T
B  H  E  Y  H  Y  W  I  P  K
V  L  Z  G  C  O  T  D  I  V
E  X  C  I  T  E  M  E  N  T
S  U  C  C  E  S  S  N  E  Q
G  C  L  O  V  E  X  C  S  A
R  Y  F  E  D  Q  V  E  S  F
```

Roller Coaster

I've heard people say that life is a roller
   coaster
Just when I feel like I've gotten closer
To something more than being a soldier
In this battlefield we call school
As we're told to live by the golden rule
When in actuality
We're surrounded by so much brutality
And expected to get straight A's
To turn in essays
And amaze
Not only the school
But a college somewhere
Who could care less
That I can't focus
That I can't progress
In school
Because I am surrounded by people so
   cruel
That I don't know where I am
What world am I living in?
When did I even learn what was on
   this exam?

BATTLEFIELD

These are the lives
Of so many kids just trying to get by
Getting used to getting F's
Because they can't take a test
When they've just been beaten by their
    classmates
And stumbled in to take their test, still out
    of breath
And how many F's can you get
Until you decide to forget
About all of those dreams
That used to seem
So possible
Well I will tell you something
They are still possible
No grade
Nor bully
Determines fully
Who you are
Who you will be
You foresee your own future
You have control of your dreams
And although it seems
Like all of those gleams
Of light
Have been put out alright

WHO

F

I can promise
That you have the ability
To reignite
And take flight
Into your future life

CHAPTER THREE

The Real You:
Out with the Old,
In with the New

I can finally say that I feel good in my own skin. That doesn't mean that I don't still have moments when I am very self-conscious. I do. Just like everyone else.

It's taken me many years to not care what other people think of me. At some point, I realized that I am special. I realized that I have a lot to offer to this planet. And I realized that I have worth. In fact, I think I was 17 when I realized this.

I went to an intensive summer acting program in New York City with 16 kids from all over the world who wanted to seriously study acting. For the first time in my life, I felt like I fit in and I made really close friends. One day we were walking around the city, hanging out and talking. In the middle of our conversation, I noticed a few of my friends looking at me. They were looking at me in a way that I can't remember ever being looked at before. They were looking at me like I was someone special.

They told me that I inspired them. They told me that I was incredible. I will never forget this because it was that one moment when I realized that I could be myself and people would still love me. And in that one moment I finally became the Real Aija.

The Real You has always been inside of you. It's the part of you that you shouldn't have to hide from the world because you are afraid of being bullied. The Real You is who you truly are with all of your imperfections. And it's who you want to be, the things you dream of doing, and the life you want to have. It's your first big leap into your new life and your new beginning.

SIX STEPPING STONES
TO THE REAL YOU

1. Have **confidence** in yourself.

2. **Accept** yourself.

3. **Embrace** your creativity.

4. **Believe** what you really believe.

5. **Become** the Real You in school.

6. Take it **step by step**.

STEPPING STONE ONE:

Have confidence in yourself

Some days you'll feel good about yourself and some days you won't. But it's important to keep up that confidence at school, especially when you are faced with bullying. These tips are here to help you boost your confidence every day. If you can learn to be confident in school, you are beginning to win the battle against the people who bully you.

Appearance

Take good care of your appearance. When we look better, we feel better.

Wear what you want and what makes you feel great. It doesn't matter what other people think is cool or what is popular in all the magazines. Take pride in your appearance and be confident.

As a young teen, I had terrible posture because all the bullying had made me ashamed of what I looked like. But I think that if I could've stood tall, held my head up, and strutted through those hallways, the bullying may actually have subsided a little bit. So I want you to try this out. Because no matter what, you deserve to be proud of yourself.

Health

Exercise! You can do jumping jacks and sit-ups in your bedroom, go for a run, join a sports team or gym, or look up different exercise videos on your computer. Exercise will make you feel better about yourself. I know it's annoying at first, but you'll get into it. Try all different kinds of exercises and find your favorite one.

Eat right. It's hard when you are surrounded by all your favorite chips and candy. But when you eat better food, you will feel better. Fast food, soda, and junk food taste great at first, but they won't help your body and mind feel good later.

Stay away from drugs and alcohol. Although you may briefly feel better for a little while taking drugs or drinking, you will always have to come down from your high. And then you will feel terrible. Not only can drugs and alcohol hurt you emotionally, they can also hurt you physically.

STEPPING STONE TWO:

Accept yourself

Accept what you're born with. Whatever your skin color, race, sexual orientation, gender identity, or ethnicity, these are parts of you that can never change. Be proud of yourself. Never be ashamed.

Accept who you are and whatever insecurities you have about yourself. Don't bully yourself. We all have limitations. It's okay to recognize that you aren't great at everything. None of us are! It's also okay to ask for help when you need it.

Accepting Your Intelligence

Do you think you're stupid based on how people treat you at school? Do you feel like you don't belong anywhere? **Here are a few suggestions for how you can recognize that you are smart in your own way:**

Tell yourself that you're smart. Remember: Being book smart and being life smart are two completely different things! I was never someone who naturally did well in school. I was always awful in math and science. It was so frustrating because no matter how hard I studied, I could never get an A or even a B. But I liked English and history. So I did my best to get good grades in those subjects. At times it was a struggle, but I'm so glad that I never stopped trying to do well in school.

Everyone has his or her own unique set of gifts. And you are no exception. So tell yourself that you're smart, talented, and important. Because I believe that you are. If you check out **Chapter 8: Creativity**, there will be plenty of sections that you may relate to.

Find something you're interested in and become a pro at it. For example, are you interested in Ancient Egypt or learning French? Do it. Spend your spare time excelling at whatever fascinates you. When you love something and you are good at it, you'll feel much better about yourself. You'll have confidence, and remember what I said earlier: If you can learn to be confident in school, you are beginning to win the battle against the people who bully you.

If you aren't doing well in a class, you don't have to feel dumb. Trying to excel will make you feel better about yourself.

WHAT YOU CAN DO . . .

* Ask a teacher for extra help with your assignments.

* Ask a peer you trust for help.

* Check out free, helpful websites for tutorials on ANY subject.

* Ask a parent, sibling, or neighbor for help.

* Set a timer (it could be for only 30 minutes a day) and make yourself study for that amount of time. It could make a HUGE difference.

* Make flash cards.

* Write a rap of the material set to your favorite song. (I've done this before and it really helped me!)

You have to be confident about who you are, no matter what insecurities you might have. This is hard and doesn't change overnight. But once you accept yourself, then dealing with being bullied becomes a lot easier to handle. Once you accept the fact that you are who you are, bullying will hurt a lot less. And, most important, you will feel good about yourself.

SURVIVAL TIP

Tell yourself this every day:

I don't deserve to be bullied. I deserve a great life. I will have a great life one day and I will do everything I can now to make that happen.

STEPPING STONE THREE:

Embrace your creativity

Creativity is an ability to make new things or think of new ideas. Creativity can be found in art, writing, sports, science, engineering, and so much more.

Creativity can make you feel good about yourself. It can transport you to a place where you can do what you love and that is the only thing that surrounds you.

When I moved to California and escaped my bullying situation, I forced myself to be creative. I started writing stories and screenplays, and acting in plays. I not only fell in love with it, but I had a lot of success because of it. I found my creativity. It not only saved me, but it healed me.

After the bullying stopped, I was left with feelings of sadness, frustration, and anger. I didn't really know what to do. But I was able to put those feelings into writing and acting. I was able to create beautiful art from my ugly experiences. It was incredible! In **Chapter 8: Creativity**, I write about how you can begin to discover your creativity.

Do What You Love
(Despite What People Think of It or You)

People are always going to judge you no matter what you do. Just let it be fuel for your fire to help you succeed. Let the judgments make you even more determined to do what you love.

Ask yourself: What do I truly want to do? I wanted to make movies in Hollywood. I had these huge dreams for a girl with no experience. People used to tell me no all the time. And my classmates told me that I would amount to nothing. This made me frustrated since I couldn't show them what I was capable of. But when I was 14, I had the opportunity to move across the country, and I was able to succeed and show people who I really was.

Throughout it all, I forced myself to remember a few things:

✴ Do not let anyone tell you NO.

✴ You can create your own destiny.

✴ Stop thinking things are impossible. Nothing is impossible.

SURVIVAL TIP

Give 100 % of yourself to what you love.

STEPPING STONE FOUR:

Believe what you really believe

Remember, no one can tell you what you really believe. What you believe comes from deep within you. Being connected to what you believe is one of the best confidence boosters that I can think of.

Some of What I Believe . . .

* I believe in standing up for other people.

* I believe in being true to myself.

* I believe in doing what makes me happy.

* I believe in treating others the way that I want to be treated.

* I believe in being honest.

* I believe in being a great friend.

* I believe in doing whatever I can to help others.

Try making a list of what you believe.

When you wake up in the morning and look in the mirror, tell yourself how special you are.

Choose three things you like about yourself and tell yourself why you like them.

Remind yourself of the incredible life you will have.

STEPPING STONE FIVE:

Become the Real You in school

Every morning before school, take three deep breaths in and out. Close your eyes and hear the voice of someone you love say something kind to you like "You're beautiful and smart" or "I'm right here for you." This person doesn't have to actually have said these words to you. I do this whenever I get stressed. I do it so often that I can actually hear the voice of the person I love. It feels like that person is right next to me. And it calms me down tremendously.

Before you go to school, visualize the day. I used to think visualizations were silly, but recently when I visualize things, good things occur. I think that if you put out good energy into the world, good things will come back to you. So visualize a day of no bullying. Visualize everyone being nice to you and even giving you compliments. Visualize good grades. Visualize whatever you would like. I can't promise you that you won't get bullied. But this is a good technique to help you see what your life can be like.

Find "You" in School

Long school days can be exhausting. And you have to deal with trying to fit in, being happy, and bullying on top of it all. I know how hard it is! But if you can find at least one thing at school that makes you happy, it will power you through your entire day.

Clubs

Find out what clubs your school offers during or after school. There are debate clubs, sports clubs, book clubs, homework clubs—and the list goes on! Types of clubs vary depending on your school, but there are always options. Talk to teachers and fellow students you trust. If you can find three clubs that seem kind of interesting to you, check them all out. It won't hurt to just try. You can always leave. If you can find two clubs that you like, join them both. That way you have more time in your day that you actually enjoy. Also, if one club is canceled, you have a backup.

When it comes to clubs, try to find people you normally don't see or talk to. Clubs can be an incredible place where you can meet new friends.

Sports

Sports are not only an amazing way to relieve stress, meet people, and feel good, but they also may make you really happy. Even if you haven't been good at the sports you've tried, there might be a new sport that you're great at.

If your school has a variety of sports teams, try out for whichever ones interest you. You can always decide to change your mind later. If you find a sport you love but you don't like the people on the team, that's okay, too! There are probably other teams in your community that you can try out for.

I was never good at group sports, but I always loved figure skating and swimming. For me, they were a great escape from the horror I dealt with during my school day.

Student Council

You could always join your student council! Whether you have a minor or major job, it could be a lot of fun. You can take part in arranging different school events or making changes to student government. It also looks great on a college application or job résumé. AND it's another place to meet people. Remember: You don't have to commit to it. Try it and decide if it's something for you!

Classes

In addition to regular academic classes, a lot of schools have interesting elective classes. Ask a teacher at your school for a list of these classes and their descriptions. Go through this list and find all of the classes that sound great to you. Talk to your advisor or an administrator about checking them out and possibly even joining them. You never know how much you might love them or who you will meet.

What Do You Want at School?

Pick the three words that will help you set the tone of your school day.

S	U	C	C	E	S	S	F	U	L
J	G	X	E	K	W	E	F	M	V
D	S	R	T	K	X	N	P	I	S
T	L	E	A	R	N	I	N	G	T
Y	C	L	K	D	S	D	P	X	N
V	V	G	D	T	E	X	Y	N	I
H	A	P	P	Y	Y	S	B	S	A
L	A	U	G	H	T	E	R	H	I
S	T	S	P	O	R	T	S	Q	P
Z	C	L	U	B	S	H	H	U	U

STEPPING STONE SIX:

Take it step by step

Just remember that your past doesn't define you. If you did or said something yesterday that you regret, it doesn't mean anything today. Be comfortable with who you really are. You can make every day a new beginning.

In school it can seem like every little bad thing that happens is the end of the world. But I promise, in a few years much of it will fade from your memory. Chances are, the people you think are judging you won't remember it either. You just need to get through this time.

I would always freak out about the littlest things in school. When I was in middle school I had a big crush on this boy. One day I wore a new outfit that I loved. These girls came up to me and told me I looked really fat in it. So I walked around the entire day with my arms crossed over my body and my head toward the ground. I avoided my crush at all costs, and when he came near me, I walked away. The rest of the year I was so self-conscious and worried about everything I wore. A few years later, I found a picture of myself in that same outfit. And I looked great! It's amazing how much we care about what people think but find it so difficult to believe in what we really think of ourselves.

I think that if you practice and embrace these Six Stepping Stones, you will feel so much better about yourself. Be patient. I know it's hard, but you are already on your way to discovering the Real You.

You Are Never Alone

We're told to deal with it
To deal with the pain that we feel
And the torment we conceal
Because it's like we're alone in this battle
Where if you tattle
You only get bullied worse
So you try to traverse
The line
Between faking a smile
And crying all of the time

I know this feeling
I know what it's like to wonder if healing
Yourself will ever be in the cards
Because everything seems so hard
You think you're walking alone in
 this tunnel
With no lights
And you're losing your reason to fight
But hold on
Because there is a light waiting for you

And once you near it
You will see
A tunnel filled
With thousands of you and me
Thinking they are walking this road alone
When actually, this whole time, they've been
    surrounded by people of their own

You
Are
Never
Alone

CHAPTER FOUR

Getting Help:
Becoming Your Own Superhero

Dear Mom and Dad,

Looking back on all my experiences with bullying, I'm sorry that I didn't communicate better with you. It's not that I didn't want to tell you—it's that I didn't know how. Being bullied is scary. Half of me felt like I must have been doing something wrong to cause it, while the other half of me knew that it wasn't my fault. But at eight years old, I didn't really know which half was right.

I remember telling you that kids were mean. I remember how badly you wanted to help my situation and all the things you tried to do to help. You went to the school to ask the administrators for assistance, you desperately tried to help me make friends, and you were always there to comfort me. You did everything you could. But so much of it was out of your control.

But I never told you exactly what was going on. I should have told you how I was feeling—that I was scared and that I had started to believe the names my bullies called me. I should have told you how every day was so dark and hard for me. But I didn't really know how. In fact, I don't think most kids or teenagers know how either.

I'm sorry that I didn't know how to completely open up to you. But I am so grateful to have had you by my side. And, at the end of the day, that gave me a feeling of safety.

Thank you, Mom and Dad, for all that you did to help me through the dark tunnel.

Love,

Aija

SURVIVAL TIP

Asking for help is not a sign of weakness.
It's a sign of strength.

Even when you feel completely isolated, there is always someone you can go to—the sometimes-tricky part is figuring out who that is. You might not find the perfect person right away, but that doesn't mean he or she isn't out there. I'm going to help you figure out how to do this.

TALKING TO PARENTS/ CAREGIVERS

The first step in dealing with bullying is to talk to your parents or caregiver. I know you might not want to do this. You might be scared or think that your parents won't understand. But try anyway.

Why You May Not Talk to Your Parents

* Many teenagers don't talk to their parents about issues because we tend to think that we can handle everything on our own.

* We want to be independent and lead our own lives.
* We expect our problems will disappear.
* We don't believe our parents can do anything to help.

But sometimes parents can change a bullying situation for the better.

Why You Should Talk to Your Parents

* They have more life experience than you. Even if they don't know much about bullying, they might be able to offer you some useful advice.
* Teachers and other school officials might be more open to talking to your parents than to you.
* Even if they don't completely understand what you are going through, it's important to know you have someone on your side. Trust me.
* Last, but not least, they LOVE YOU!

I understand that it's scary to talk to your parents. You might feel like you did something wrong or like you should be ashamed of the fact that you are being bullied. But that is FALSE. You did NOTHING wrong. **You have NOTHING to be ashamed of.**

What Do I Tell My Parents?

Your parents might not know exactly what bullying is. It could be helpful to explain it to them. Check out the definition at the beginning of this book or look for resources online.

You should tell your parents exactly what is going on. Whether it is really bad or only sometimes upsetting, give your parents all of the details. Be open with them. Ask your parents for their help, because you need it.

How Do I Tell My Parents?

You actually have several options on how to tell your parents. There is no right or wrong way. It's about what makes YOU feel most comfortable.

The "Sit-Down"

If you feel you are able to, ask your parents to sit down for a talk. Find a time that works for all of you and isn't in the middle of a busy day. Try an evening or a weekend. Here is how you can start:

> Hi Mom/Dad,
>
> I need to talk to you. I'm not in trouble or anything, but I need your advice on something that is really upsetting me. When can we talk about this?

I know how scary it is to bring up bullying. So break the news in the way that makes YOU feel the most comfortable. When you've found a good time to get your parents' attention, tell them what's going on. Looking back, I wish that I had said something like this to my parents:

Hi Mom/Dad,

People are being really mean to me. I thought it would pass. I was shaking it off for a while because I know that's what you would tell me to do. But it really hurts. Especially when [name your bullies] call me names like [tell them specifics]. I don't have any friends and I feel very upset. It is affecting my grades and my attention. I really need your help because I am having a very hard time.

Hopefully, your parents will have some words of advice. Or maybe they will need a little time to think about what to do. Remember: This is a very new problem for your parents, too. They also might not react in a way that feels helpful the first time you talk about it. They might think this issue isn't a big deal and that it's "kids being kids." They might think that you can or should handle it on your own.

But you should continue to talk to them. You can say something like, "I understand you think that I can handle it myself, but I have tried. I am really sad and can't stand being at school. I think I need you to help me find a better way to deal with this."

If you don't feel the conversation was successful, don't lose hope. Sometimes it takes more than one conversation. Give your parents a few days to digest your first conversation and then try again. Also, think about writing down the exact bullying events and sitting down with your parents to discuss it again. Tell them that, according to Whitehouse.gov, 13 million American kids are bullied every year. This isn't strange or unusual. Feel free to do a little research. Sometimes facts help parents understand.

SURVIVAL TIP

No matter how angry or frustrated you feel, do not retaliate against your bullies with violence.

Violence can get you in a lot of trouble, make situations much worse, and can even put you in more danger. However, if someone hurts you physically, you should do whatever you need to do to get out of the situation and get help.

Writing to Your Parents

If you're too afraid to talk to your parents face-to-face, that's okay. I can relate! You can always write them a letter.

Hi Mom/Dad,

I need to talk to you about something, but I get scared every time I try. I have been having a really hard time at school. Kids are being really mean to me and bullying me. It happens all the time and it is distracting me from school, making me sad, and leaving me feeling alone.

I really need your help to figure out this problem. Can we talk about it sometime?

Love,

[Your Name]

Other Ways to Tell Your Parents

You can even get creative with the way you talk to your parents about what's going on. You can draw a picture, do an art project, or write a song or a poem. There are lots of ways to tell your parents. If I could go back to the time I was bullied, I think I would have written them a letter or a poem. Sometimes it's easier to speak through the written word rather than with your voice.

Five Good Things That Might Come from Talking to Your Parents

★ Your parents can go to your school and find out the school's official policy on bullying. Then they can work with the school to stop the bullying. Your school may be more receptive to listening to your parents than to you alone.

★ Your parents can find you resources in your community where you can talk to other kids who are dealing with bullying.

★ Your parents can decide if you need someone to talk to, like a therapist or counselor.

★ Your parents can help you to find new friends through clubs, after-school activities, sports teams, community events, etc.

★ Your parents will now know that you are having a hard time and can be right by your side to support you.

What If My Parents Don't Help Me?

If your parents are not willing or not able to help you with this situation, then you need to find another adult to talk to. Come up with a list of the five most trustworthy adults in your life. The list could be made up of relatives, neighbors, teachers, coaches, etc. Jot down your list, figuring out who the first person should be. If he or she doesn't work out, go to the next person.

TALKING TO TEACHERS

Most schools have official policies about the best way to report bullying. I would suggest finding out what this policy is right away and talking to the appropriate school administrators. You should include your parents in this conversation, too.

I remember being afraid to ask my teachers for help, because I thought it might make things a lot worse. But that's not always true. Teachers can be a big help. First, find a teacher you feel safe with. Who is most trustworthy? Who is the kindest to you? Who seems like a good problem solver? Then, I would suggest approaching him or her after class, during lunch, or during a free time. Ask this teacher if you could talk privately about a problem you are having. You might say something like this:

I have something I need to talk to you about, but I have to make sure that it stays between you and me right now. I'm nervous about the other kids finding out.

I'm having a lot of problems with bullying. Kids like [say the name] are really mean to me and they say things to me like [tell them specifics]. I'm afraid to participate in class or even walk in the hallways. It's distracting from my focus in school and I think it might affect my grades. Can you help me with this? I feel alone and sad.

This might start a dialogue that makes things better. Maybe the teacher will include other administrators or your parents in the conversation. But there's a chance that this won't change anything either. If that's the case, find another teacher or go to someone else on your top five list. **Don't stop trying.** You could also have another conversation at a later date with the same teacher. Perhaps bring additional details about specific bullying situations. **IT WILL GET BETTER, especially the more you reach out for help.**

Five Good Things That Might Come from Talking to a Teacher

✳ Your teacher can help you find out the school's policy about bullying. Then he or she can keep an eye on you and possibly intervene if you are being bullied.

✳ Your teacher might talk to other teachers or your principal about the situation. They might be able to talk to the kid or kids bullying you or to their parents. Your teachers could even set up a meeting between you, your parents, the kid bullying you, and his/her parents for all of you to talk together.

✳ Your teacher could come up with alternative ways for you to make friends and be happy at school. He or she might know of some other really cool kids to introduce you to. You never know what ideas your teacher might have!

* Your teacher could explain the situation to your parents (if you feel comfortable with this).

* Your teacher will now know that you are having a hard time and be able to talk to you about it. Having someone on your side, who understands you, can be a big comfort.

What If My Teacher Doesn't Help Me?

When I was younger, I spent so many years going to my teachers and finding no results. They wouldn't help me and they didn't understand what bullying was. But then, one day when I was a bit older, something incredible happened. There was a bullying situation that was very upsetting and scary for me. I had no choice but to go to one of my teachers and tell her what was going on.

I went to her after class, when no one else was around, and told her what was happening. I burst into tears and she listened to everything I was saying. She hugged me and said, "I am going to fix this situation, Aija." And guess what? She did. She found a way to quietly alert the other teachers to the problem. These teachers made sure that I did not need to cross paths with the bully. They were always watching, and if I needed them, they were right there. I spent so many years not getting help from teachers, but I was really just waiting for the right one. She is a hero and there are other teachers like her out there. Keep asking for help until you find your hero teacher!

If you cannot find help from a particular teacher, then

you should seek out another school official to talk to. This could include a different teacher, a school counselor or nurse, or the principal.

Say that you have tried to get help but you are not getting anywhere. Never give up. Do not lose hope. You deserve help and you will get it once you find the right person.

SURVIVAL TIP

If you are still not getting the help you need, I promise you that there is still help out there! See the Hotline page at the back of the book for lots of ideas!

Finding the light at the end of the tunnel will not happen overnight. Think of it like this: You are walking through a dark tunnel. It might feel like you're searching for that light forever and that it will never come. But you aren't alone. When you get closer to the light, it will illuminate the tunnel. Suddenly, you will see there are other people there, too. They were always there; you just couldn't see them. There are other kids who are bullied, family members, friends, teachers—all people who you can talk to and even some who can help. You just never noticed them before. I promise this will happen one day. Be patient. Keep trying. It will get better.

I Knew Fear

I knew fear when I lost all hope
In the world and in trying to cope
With the brutality that became a normality
With the backstabbers
And the games
I tried to figure out who to blame
Was it my fault?
Was it fate?
Or my weight
Or even the fact that I wanted to create
A life for myself
Where I could be the person
Who I was too ashamed to be at school
So I feared the world
Because who would I ever be if I wasn't "cool"

I knew fear when I believed
What these kids were saying to me
When they told me I wouldn't achieve
Or succeed
Or be anything I wanted to be
Because I was a nothing
And I was disgusting

69

So I feared myself
Because maybe Beauty and the Beast
    wasn't just a book on a shelf
I knew fear when the kids I thought
    were my friends
Betrayed me to such an extent
That I questioned humanity
But mostly myself
Why was I the only one sitting at a table
    by herself?
I spent so much time alone
That I felt like I may be living in the
    Arctic Zone
And any time someone spoke to me
I jumped
Because I had been so used to being
    an absentee
Or guaranteed bullying

But suddenly I realized
That it was my fate
To be catapulted with words
Tortured and harassed without being deferred
To an easier life

Even though it took many years to see
   the light
At the end of the tunnel

LIGHT

I had to suffer
To realize that I am tougher
Than who I thought I was

I am better
Than who they told me to be

And I am braver
Than I could ever see

me

CHAPTER FIVE

Fear:
The Dark Tunnel

We all have fears. I had a lot when I was being bullied. In 7th grade I was terrified to participate in class. I had a lisp, and whenever I spoke I was bullied by the students and even some teachers. They would mock the way I spoke, laugh hysterically, or make mean comments. It was humiliating! It took me a long time to get help for the lisp, and in that time my fears affected my grades, confidence, and happiness. I had other fears, too. I was afraid of being picked last for a group activity, running during gym, not being invited to parties, and the list goes on. **But it's all about how we deal with our fears.** I dealt with my fears about speaking in public, and now I think it's pretty amazing that I want to pursue a career in acting and that I love public speaking. Who would have guessed that the little girl who was too afraid to speak would later use her voice to tell important stories?

Have you ever been told to "not be afraid"? I have. Have you ever tried to not be afraid when you really were? I have.

Accepting your fears is how you control your fears.

We are always told from a very young age that we shouldn't be scared of answering a question wrong or going on a class trip. But I disagree. I think that it's normal to be afraid sometimes. I think that it's okay to have fears. I also believe that you can control your fears by understanding and accepting them. It's all about figuring out the right way to deal with how you are feeling.

THE HAUNTING

Have you ever had a thought or a moment that played over and over in your mind? It's almost like you can't press PAUSE and your brain is stuck on REWIND and PLAY. This is what I call the haunting.

The haunting is the never-ending, rapid speed at which your thoughts pick at and attack your mind throughout the entire day. It is the constant going over and over and over everything you said, did, heard, felt, saw—it is the endless attack that is bullying. Even when people aren't bullying you, their past attacks are haunting you.

So in a way every morning was a haunting of the past day for me. And this is a terrible thing because it only amps up your nerves and anxiety for the coming day. It creates a shadow of negativity for a day that hasn't even occurred yet. You can think of it as a ghost that follows you around. But you may think, *How can I possibly get rid of this ghost? Why is it following me?* In one word, it is this—**FEAR.**

FEAR OF LONELINESS

Do you feel like you have no friends? Are you alone almost all of the time? This is not weird at all. I can totally understand since I spent so many of my years in school alone and without friends. I can also tell you that there are ways to deal with this. Here are a few tips:

* **Tell yourself that this is temporary.** You will not always be alone. You will not always be friendless. I promise you this. When I was being bullied, I thought I would be friendless forever. I couldn't see how there would be any other way of living. But change was possible. I did make friends through after-school activities, summer classes, and finding people with mutual interests. I now have friends who I hang out with all the time and they are there for me no matter what.

* **Expand your social horizons.** It seems hard and scary, but it's worth it. Go out to the parts of your town that attract kids your age like a coffee shop,

mall, bookstore, or community clubs. Be yourself. Walk into a space, look around, and see if there is something you can learn or be interested in.

* **Fill the gap of loneliness with something you enjoy.** Whether this is writing, art, academics, sports, anything—dive into what you love. Maybe even create a long-term project. That is exactly what I did. I started writing this book when I had no friends and was very lonely. Not only will this fill the gap, but it will also leave you with a finished product that you can be proud of.

HOW TO HELP WITH YOUR FEARS

Talk to a friend, family member, or someone you care about for a half hour every day about whatever you want. Also:

Exercise/do sports

Go to therapy

Talk to your "Future You" (see page 78)

Pick one thing you love or like and focus on it for an hour a day

Go outside/go for a walk
(one of my favorites)

Draw

Write

Act (one of my favorites), sing, dance

Make a list of goals for your future

Read a book

Listen to music

Watch a TV show or movie (one of my favorites)

Cook or bake something

Become spiritual or religious
(if you feel it may help you)

Find a yoga tutorial online

Play with an animal

Treat yourself to something special

Take a hot shower/bath

Take a nap

If you're feeling **A LOT** of fear or anger inside yourself,
here are some suggestions:

Take deep breaths

Take a pillow and hit the couch
with it as hard as you can

Stomp and scream "No! It's not my fault! I don't
deserve this!" as loud as you want, while in a
private place

Place bubble wrap on the floor and stomp on it

Lie on the sofa or your bed and kick your
legs in the air and shake your head

Punch a pillow or the mattress on
your bed as many times as you like

However, if these activities are making you feel angrier, then try:

Talking to an adult about what you are feeling

Writing down your feelings and frustrations

Taking a relaxing shower or bath

Exercising

Going for a walk

CREATING YOUR FUTURE YOU

I've always been a dreamer, and creating my Future Me is how I dealt with my fears. I hope it helps you!

Think of yourself in 10 years. Think of your dream life, dream job, dream boyfriend or girlfriend, dream wardrobe, dream appearance, anything. I want you to visualize your Future You. You are not only perfect in every way you want to be, but you are also very strong. **The Future You is the part of you that has already overcome bullying.** The Future You has more life experience and is more confident than you are now. The Future You is going to help you get through this.

Every time you are scared, have your Future You talk you through it, like this:

> **Aija:** I'm so scared to see the kids who bully me today. I wish I could just run away.

> **Future Aija:** It's all going to be okay. Calm down. Take a deep breath. In 10 years, you aren't even going to care about them. You've just got to make it through today.

DAY IN THE LIFE: TALKING TO THE FUTURE YOU

The Future You is already inside you, so you might as well start speaking to this new person. Imagine that you're speaking to yourself in the future.

6:30 AM

> **Aija:** I never want to leave my bed. I don't want to deal with another day of this. Maybe I can fake sick?

> **Future Aija:** Aija, it's going to be okay. I can see how amazing your life is in the future. Now, get out of bed. We're going to get through this day together.

7:00 AM

Aija: I look terrible in everything. I have nothing to wear.

Future Aija: Whoa there. You have plenty to wear. You're just feeling not too hot about yourself this morning. Wear something you feel comfortable in.

8:00 AM

Aija: I don't want to get out of the car. I can't do this. The kids who bully me are going to be so mean.

Future Aija: Chill out, girl. If you think it's going to be a bad day, it will be a bad day. It's nice out. Let's try to make the day good.

8:30 AM

Aija: I hate this class. All these people are so mean. They're all staring at me.

Future Aija: Yeah, this class might be really boring and the people aren't exactly sweethearts. But it's only an hour more of this. Try to focus. And no, they aren't staring at you, you're just nervous and you feel like they are. Remember, Aija, that everyone has problems.

12:00 PM

Aija: I don't know what to do. Every time I sit down with people, they move. I just want someone to eat lunch with me.

Future Aija: Honey, in the future you're going to have a line of people wanting to eat lunch with you. Right now, you just have to get through this lunch hour. Maybe let's eat outside? That a better view than these people's faces.

3:00 PM

Aija: I'm so bad at sports. I can't even run. The kids in gym class are going to bully me.

Future Aija: Well, you can't be good at everything. Just pretend all of the other people aren't there. This class will be over soon.

5:00 PM

Aija: I just want to be left alone. I don't want to do homework.

Future Aija: I know, sweetie. But if you do your homework and the other stuff you need to do, then you'll be able to do something fun or relax. You're not too far away. Just gotta do a few more things.

Aija: All I can think about is how mean they all are and how much they hate me. I just want to go to sleep. Why can't my mind stop thinking?

Future Aija: Because you're allowing it to think. You deserve a wonderful night's rest. Tell your brain to stop thinking or count down from 100. You need your rest, Aija.

Your Future You is always there for you, even when no one else is. As you go about your day, imagine your Future You standing right behind you. Your Future You is always watching to make sure you're okay and protecting you when you need protection. Your Future You will never leave you, as long as you keep dreaming, keep believing, and keep needing him or her.

Alone and Lost

Have you ever felt so alone
To the point where you believe you're in a
    combat zone
Because how could you be so alone
In a world of billions
How could no one want to talk to you
A normal civilian
How could no one acknowledge you
When your mama says you're one in
    a million

Have you ever felt so lost
That you're not sure what territory
    you've crossed into
Are you in this world
Or another
You just feel smothered
By your life
So you wish every night
For guidance or freedom

Don't you worry
Because you won't always be lonely
You'll find that one person

Who will never leave your side
Who will hold you when you cry
And you'll find yourself
In this world
You'll find your way
And learn to start your day
With a smile so bright
Because you will be able to sleep at night
And those moments that haunt you
Will no longer taunt you

You will see
You'll be set free

Free

✦ CHAPTER SIX ✦

Battlefield Scenarios:
Surviving in the Trenches

I can promise you that middle school or high school will end and none of the people who have hurt you will matter to you anymore. That's just the way life works. But how you do academically will stick with you for a long time. It'll help or hurt your future.

Do NOT let being bullied define your success in school. It's definitely hard to focus when you're being bullied, but put all of your energy into the areas where you want to succeed.

Your success in life is what will matter in the long run. The frustrating comments that your peers make about you will either be forgotten or be fuel for the fire that will make you stronger and more determined.

Since the day I started getting bullied, I became terrified of participating in class. I didn't want to stand out. I didn't want to answer questions. I didn't even want to do homework. I was so afraid of what my classmates would say about me. But one day I realized that I was only hurting myself by doing badly in school. So I slowly started to be a student rather than just a kid counting the minutes until school ended. I became a person with a voice and opinions rather than just another kid who sat through class without speaking or paying attention. And I did really well. I even got accepted to my top-choice college. **At the end of the day, the only person who can rob you of your dreams is you. Remember, success is a gift that you give yourself.**

To succeed academically, I knew I had to try to avoid the kids who were bullying me. So I started to be on the lookout for places where they didn't go. I found the theater (which I fell in love with), I found a bathroom (which was basically abandoned), I found a little garden (where no one went), and the nurse's office (which I frequented every day).

I made sure to go to these places during the roughest times of each day. When I wanted to avoid bullying, I knew where to go. I was safe there. And I was the happiest that I could be at school.

I also became friends with someone who was not having the best time in school either. We weren't close friends, but she was someone I could hang out with during school. It made me happier. I wasn't always alone. I had someone to sit with at lunch and someone who was by my side if I was being bullied. This is what I call the "wingman" later in this chapter.

There are other things you can do to improve your situation at school that don't involve avoiding the people who make you unhappy. Why not talk to your teachers or school administrators about the problem of bullying in general? Perhaps you can brainstorm ideas on how to prevent bullying at your school. You might also ask if there could be more supervision in the hallways or at lunch.

Or what about starting an anonymous poll about bullying? This might be a great way to see just how many kids are in your position. Then you can take this information back to your teachers and talk about ways to improve things at your school.

Or why not start a Kindness Club or a Volunteering Club? This will help make your school or community a better place—and you might make great friends in the process! There are so many ways for you to get involved, make friends, and even stand up to bullying.

PREPARING FOR BATTLE IN SCHOOL

To help me deal with the bullying, I created the battlefield scenarios. They're basically an overview of bullying situations and the best tactics to have ready for each scenario.

Whether you are having trouble in the hallways before school begins or in the locker room right before gym, the battlefield scenarios give you a basic road map to find the right solution to your problem.

But don't forget your first resources are your parents and teachers. Look back at **Chapter 4: Getting Help** for more ideas on how to get their support.

Building Your Battle Plan

Think of all of the places you go and the people you usually pass at school. You need to create a battle plan for every place you go.

Knowing "the Five P's" will help you get ready to make your battle plan.

People:

You need to take mental notes of the usual people you are around in various places. Who is usually around (whether you talk to them, don't talk to them, like them, or dislike them)?

Place:

You need to find an escape route in every place you go.

Partner:

You need to find an ally (either a peer or a teacher) in every place you go.

Path:

You need to try every road to your destination and choose the best one for you.

Program:

You need to customize your routine to fit your happiness.

SURVIVAL TIP

You need to be sure to practice
your battle plan once a day.

When you are face-to-face with someone
who bullies you, everything happens so quickly.
You need to be on your game and ready for whatever
may happen. Getting into the routine of this
battle plan will help you with that.

**Aija's Example Battle Plan for 8:00 AM
Math (Classroom 121)**

People:

John, Bob, Ariel, Sam, Kate, Matthew, Dylan,
Jessica, Maria

Place:

Right wall door, door behind Ms. King's desk

Partner:

Ariel and Ms. King

Path:

Through the middle school hallway (it's a longer path but the middle schoolers are nicer), behind the French classroom (because there are bullies in that class and when I pass by I get scared), and down the staircase (because I never see the bullies go that way).

Program:

I like this class because there aren't too many mean people, but if there is a problem, I will talk to my teacher.

Now that you have developed your battle plan, visualize it. See it in action.

The Hallways

The hallways are difficult to negotiate, so you need to have a plan. Here are some reasons why:

Basic Problems: The kids who bully you have full view of everyone and their ability to target is endless. There usually isn't any supervision in the hallways. There is typically a lot of chaos, too.

Basic Solutions: Minimize the time you spend in the hallways and move quickly. This is also true for any big, open area where you can be targeted with no adults watching.

Before School

Every school is different, so every hallway scenario is different. Think about your school. What time of day do the people who bully you travel through the hallways? Let's say it's in the morning, before school begins. It really helps to avoid problems before they start.

If for some reason you have to go through the hallways, pick a side to stay on and stick to it. If you feel more comfortable toward the right-hand lockers, immerse yourself in a group of people and walk quickly. The less time you spend wandering around the halls the better.

Come to school a few minutes earlier one day and take a look at the crowd in the hallways. Are there fewer people? Are there more? Are the kids who give you a hard time there? If not, you may want to start coming to school a few minutes earlier to avoid any problems.

During School

The hallways can become a crazy place during a school day. That's why if there are alternative routes, you should take them and avoid the hallways. But if you have to stick with the hallways, that's fine, too. Keep an eye on the varying levels of craziness—which passing periods are more insane than others? You can customize your battle plan based on this, too.

After School

The hallways can be dangerous after school as well. Sometimes only a few people can be found in the hallways at this time. This is dangerous because you can be bullied and have absolutely no ally and no escape route. Try to be with a large group of people, a friend, or a teacher.

The Classroom

What can be so exhausting about being bullied in school is that adults still expect you to get good grades. It can be really hard to avoid bullying and do well in school at the same time. We're going to try to master both together.

Participating, Being a Good Student, and Getting A's
To avoid getting bullied, you can stop participating in class. But you'll also be risking your grade and chance of succeeding in the class. This is where you just have to look honestly at your situation.

Is the bullying not terrible but you're still afraid?

Is the bullying tolerable enough that you can participate sometimes?

Is the bullying so bad that you'll get harassed if you participate?

If you are being bullied for participating in class, be sure to tell your teacher. If he or she doesn't listen, talk to your principal or guidance counselor. If you can write down the specific date and time of the incidents and the frequency, it will be helpful.

I also suggest reading or rereading **Chapter 5: Fear**. It's a whole chapter dedicated to your fears and how to overcome them.

The Lunchroom

It almost seems like there isn't a place where you can go to escape the bullying, right? Like it follows you everywhere? And when you have time at lunch to relax and eat, you can't even do that because you are being bullied.

You need a wingman—someone who will be there for you in a bad situation. This person doesn't have to be interested in all the things that you are or even be your best friend—he or she just has to make you feel safe. Try to find someone to become friends with so you aren't alone. Why? Because it is harder to be targeted if you have a friend with you.

The Outside

How about dining outside if the weather permits? You may be able to avoid bullying this way. Find a spot that is in clear view of security or administrative offices. You can always bring a book, notepad, phone, or computer to keep you busy.

Find something that you love to do and put your energy into that instead.

Avoiding the "Sit-and-Move"

The "sit-and-move" is when you sit down at a table and then everyone else gets up and moves. I can't tell you how many times I have been a victim of this. It's an awful feeling, and you're left not knowing what to do since you likely got no explanation, or someone said something silly like, "Well, it's a free country. I can move whenever I want." Bottom line: This is insulting and hateful. And you, someone who is special and incredible, do not need to subject yourself to this nonsense.

SURVIVAL TIP

If you're a victim of the "sit-and-move," listen closely:

Do not get up and follow the people who have left you.

Brush it off and join people who will respect you, or stay strong and stay put. You can always pull out a book to keep you busy.

Lunchtime Jobs

There are many tasks great and small that need to get done during the school day. Teachers and administrators are always looking for someone to work in the front office, file papers, prepare a classroom, etc. So volunteer your lunchtime; just be sure to pack a lunch and make time to eat. These types of jobs can be long-term and are a wonderful tactic for avoiding unwanted incidents. You also never know who you may meet.

The Locker Room

The locker room is by far one of the easiest places to get bullied in. It's easy to feel uncomfortable in the locker room. So a group of teenagers all undressing and all feeling uncomfortable is not a good situation. Always remember that everyone is self-conscious about something.

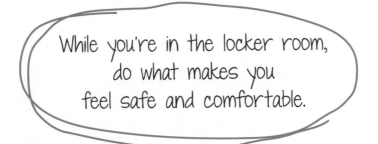

While you're in the locker room, do what makes you feel safe and comfortable.

Possible Solutions:

* Change in the bathroom stall.

* Change quickly.

* Get to the locker room early.

* Find a different part of the locker room to change in.

* Change in the school bathroom versus the gym bathroom.

* Practice changing your clothes at home very quickly. This way you will be super fast in the locker room.

Gym Class

Gym class is rough because you can be bullied for not being strong in athletics. And skipping gym class is a bad solution. It can lead to detention and hurt your grades.

I was constantly bullied in gym class and I was miserable. I wasn't the most athletic kid, so people would bully me for being a slower runner or not catching the ball. I was ALWAYS the last person to get picked for a team. Sometimes kids would even go out of their way to trip me and make me fall. At the time, I wasn't comfortable dealing with my lack of athletic skills nor did I understand how I could learn to laugh off the fact that I wasn't good at sports. Just because you may not be as athletic as another student doesn't mean that you need to get down on yourself.

SURVIVAL TIP

Own your unathletic nature.

Don't be afraid to make fun of yourself. This might make the kids who bully you uncomfortable and leave you alone. Or they will find it funny and leave you alone. If that doesn't work, then just do your best. Try to improve and have fun along the way.

Physical bullying can be disguised as accidents, whether in gym class or in any other part of school. If someone is repeatedly tripping you, hitting you, or knocking you down and you think it's bullying, you must do whatever you need to do to get away from the situation so you can tell an adult. Never deal with it by yourself! If you don't get immediate action, then go straight to your favorite teacher or the principal. I don't mean when class is finished, I mean right then and there. Bullying can escalate, and no matter what anyone says to you, you have the right to protect yourself. Remember, you are special and important and should never be attacked!

BATTLEFIELD SCENARIOS FOR OUTSIDE OF SCHOOL

Now that you know how to be prepared at school, let's take a look at how to be prepared in social situations. You absolutely must ask yourself the following questions and understand the tactics before making the decision to visit a peer's home. Bullying can escalate into much more serious issues, so you have to be careful. This is all part of preparing your battlefield scenarios and you can never know when or where a dangerous situation may take place.

The Questions

* What do you really think about the person whose house it is?

* Does this person actually like you or do you just want him or her to like you?

* What area is the house in? (Is it safe? Are there a lot of people around?)

* Will the parents be home?

* Who else might be at the house?
* Will there be drugs and alcohol that will affect the behavior of the kids?

The Tactics

Create your battle map of the house.

When walking up to the house, pay attention to your surroundings.

If you drive, be sure to park right in front of the house. It's helpful if you don't have to rely on anyone else for transportation.

If you don't drive, make sure someone you feel safe with drops you off, whether a neighbor, family member, or friend. Have this person on call to pick you up as well.

Give the address and phone number of the house to two people you feel safe with. This can be a parent, sibling, or neighbor, for example.

When walking into the house, notice if you feel comfortable or uncomfortable. Are the parents home? Are there alcohol, drugs, or weapons in plain sight? Is there a good boy-to-girl ratio? Are there kids who bully you there?

SURVIVAL TIP

Trust your gut.

If you don't feel safe, leave immediately.
You need to have full confidence in yourself.

Be Safe

Even if you are at a party with your friends, you still need to be careful. The list below is not about bullying. But bullying can escalate into other very serious issues and it's important to be aware of the situations you put yourself in. Repeat this mental checklist to yourself whenever you are at a party to prevent a bad situation from happening to you.

* If I get a drink, I have to see exactly what goes into it.
* Alcohol and drugs can make me a target to be taken advantage of.
* I can't put my drink down, even if I am watching it.
* I need to always have an exit strategy.
* Some people can be violent and crazy at parties. Stay away from those people.
* Don't go into secluded rooms.
* Don't get in a car with anyone.
* Trust yourself and your gut feeling.

SURVIVAL TIP

The moment that you step into someone's house for a hangout or a party, you need to see how you feel.

Check out the three levels below:

Green: You are probably in a relatively safe situation. You feel good about who you are with, where you are, and what you are doing.

Yellow: There are a few things about the situation that are making you nervous. Everything is going okay, but remember, things can always change, so you still need to be on your game.

Red: You are in danger. You don't feel good about who you are with, where you are, or what you are doing. Get out and get to a safe place! Things happen very quickly and your safety is your number one priority.

The Battle Is Won from the Inside Out

If you're being bullied and are scared to start the process of dealing with it, please remember that success and victory take time. **A war isn't won overnight.** But in the end, it only matters who you are within and how you are going to make a better life for yourself. If you want to fight back verbally, then do it. If you don't want to fight back, then don't. Just know that it isn't about what you say or do, but it's about who you are and who you want to be. You need to treat yourself the way you want to be treated. This battle is won from the inside out.

Broken and Bruised

I've been broken
Bruised
Stabbed and subdued
Submerged in darkness
Told there would be no light
Robbed of my rights
Put down in plain sight
But I've risen from the darkness
Shined brighter than any light . . .

CHAPTER SEVEN

#CYBERBULLYiNG: Pressing Delete

Halloween of my freshman year in high school was one of the scariest days of my life. It wasn't scary because of a haunted house or a ghost—it was scary because in one moment, my perception of my life changed greatly. I was at my new school and life seemed much better. I wasn't being bullied and I had made some new friends. It was lunchtime and I was dressed in my Halloween costume. Suddenly, I got a text message from a girl at my old school in New York. The text included a picture of one of her classmates whom I had never met. This girl was dressed up as me for Halloween. She paraded around my old school with a big sign on her neck bearing my name. The next few moments were a blur and it seemed like my life went into slow motion. I couldn't feel anything. Feeling would have been too painful.

I was in shock. I went up to my group of friends and showed them the flood of text messages, Facebook messages, and comments that were disgusting and humiliating. Just when I thought the situation was at its worst, my "friends" laughed at me and walked away.

In a matter of minutes, I had been impersonated and humiliated 3,000 miles away by a girl I didn't even know, my new "friends" had all abandoned me, and the Band-Aid had been ripped off my new life in California. I had been sucked back into the bullying for round two.

And that is when I truly knew fear. I had never felt so alone, so despised, and so lost in all of my life. I didn't fear the kids who did this to me. I feared the world and I feared myself. I could not understand why I was chosen to be a dartboard for someone else's amusement. I could not understand why the bullying followed me to California. **I was terrified because I was in a pitch-black tunnel and I couldn't see the light.**

#CYBERTYPES

There are many types of cyberbullying. Learn them all to know what you are dealing with.

Harassment
Actions that threaten or embarrass a person—posting rumors, threats, or embarrassing information on social media sites.

Impersonation
Pretending to be someone else on social media in order to bully, make fun of, or spread personal information.

Photographs

Using photographs to bully or humiliate you is another form of cyberbullying.

Taking nude or degrading photographs in a locker room or bathroom and threatening to share these embarrassing photos is also a form of cyberbullying and it is illegal.

Websites, Blogs, Polls, Hacking

The creation of websites, blogs, and polls is another form of cyberbullying. The spreading of rumors online, posting personal information, using information that was shared in private and making it public, sending viruses and spyware, and hacking your computer are forms of cyberbullying, too.

Happy-Slapping

"Happy-Slapping" is filming a bullying incident and posting it online or sharing it with other people for viewing.

I wrote this chapter to help you protect yourself. Cyberbullying impacted me maybe more than any of the face-to-face bullying. I don't want it to happen to you. Please take this quiz first to see where you are in the cyberworld. Then read the rest of the chapter to learn how to protect yourself.

#CYBERSELF PART 1

Do you get frequent messages that say mean things?

Yes / No / Maybe

Do the messages make you feel bad?

Yes / No / Maybe

Do people talk about you (in a mean way) online?

Yes / No / Maybe

If you answered "Yes" or "Maybe" to these questions, you might be dealing with cyberbullying. You should read this chapter and figure out what you need to do to protect yourself online. Don't wait. I know how dangerous and hurtful cyberbullying is and I don't want you to be affected by it.

#CYBERCRAVE

So why do you continue to obsess over social media when it hurts you? If you aren't invited to a party and all of the pictures are posted, that's hurtful. If everyone likes one person's photo and no one likes yours, that's hurtful, too. Think about it. It may have hurt you and you don't even realize it. That's where the problems can get dangerous. You can get depressed and feel very lonely, frustrated, and confused. But you probably continue to wander around cyberspace anyway. That is because we live to feel connected. If we delete all of our social media, we will be separated from the rest of the cyberworld. That's a bad feeling—especially since you're probably feeling pretty alone already.

Why does cyberbullying feel more destructive than other types of bullying?

The answer is simple: As long as you are online, you cannot seem to escape your bullies.

With all the time we spend online, it's no wonder that cyberbullying is so prevalent. It is easy, can be anonymous, and the bullies know exactly where to find you. Despite everything that I have just mentioned, we still gravitate toward social media. Why? Maybe we are lonely and want a friend. Or maybe we are afraid of being rejected in real life but find it easier to be a social butterfly online. People may use social media to fill a void, but that can be dangerous. You are a member of the cybersociety, but that doesn't mean that the cybersociety will protect you. If you use the Internet and social media as a tool to cover your loneliness or fear, you will always be lonely because nothing will ever be enough. If you got 50 likes on your Facebook profile picture and someone else got 200 likes on theirs, that 50 won't seem like much anymore. We might keep going back to social media hoping to feel better about ourselves, but that confidence can never really come from there. Confidence must come from within. **We are addicted to having and knowing everything first—information, clothing, music, invitations to parties, and so many other things. In our culture, this is what determines if we are cool or not.** And most of us are afraid of being uncool. But this lifestyle prevents you from being the real you.

#CYBERSELF PART 2

Do you check social media (phone or computer) all day long?

Yes / No / Maybe

Are you checking social media to see if you got likes, comments, requests, or messages?

Yes / No / Maybe

Do you feel upset or sad when other people get a lot of likes and you don't?

Yes / No / Maybe

If you answered "Yes" or "Maybe" to most of these questions, you may be using social media as a tool to boost your self-esteem. Maybe that's because you have friends, feel lonely, or don't know how to deal with bullying. This can be dangerous. You need to find alternative ways to feel better about yourself. Don't worry—it is possible! I have gone through this, too. I remember the time when social media was an escape for me and I felt safe behind my computer. I felt far away from the people bullying me. But in truth, I was closer to them than ever. They were just one click away from being able to cyberbully me.

FILL THE #CYBERCRAVE

You are you. But is there another you on social media? Even if you have the same friends and talk about the same things (on social media), you might be a different person. You may be more daring. You may be more open. And that's okay. But how do you feel when you're not on social media? Do you feel an emptiness inside you? Do you feel incomplete? You must find out who you really are. When you log off social media, you give yourself the room to discover who you really are and what you really love. I went off social media for a few months in 9th grade. During this time, something incredible happened. I wrote several screenplays and even won a competition in an international film festival! I discovered who I was and what I loved because I had time to focus on myself rather than on social media. Who knows what you might find if you take a break from social media!

Benefits of Being Off Social Media

* You might discover what you love when you give yourself a break from (or stop using) social media.

* If you accept who you are, you might become less attached to social media. Then cyberbullying may affect you less.

* You can become your own best friend by connecting to yourself. If you become your own best friend, you'll never be disappointed. You will always be there for yourself even when no one else is there for you. So get to know who you truly are. Deep down, what do you love? What do you dislike? Where are you happiest? Love yourself always.

How to Fill the #CyberCrave

* Connect (face-to-face) with one person you love and care about every day. This could be for just a few minutes.

* Spend time at coffee shops, bookstores, or other places kids your age go. Feel free to go up and talk to people your age. Be your true self. And be that person around other people. You'll also feel less lonely that way.

* Find a hobby that introduces you to a new social circle in the community.

* Join a nonprofit organization or club in your community.

* Get a job. Who knows who you will meet?

WHO IS YOUR #CYBERBULLY?

You might not even know how you're affected while the cyberattacks are occurring. But they will affect you. One of the biggest issues that comes with cyberbullying is numbers. Since it's so easy to create anonymous accounts, it is impossible to know if the cruel messages you receive are from one person or 50 people. When social media is anonymous, it makes us feel like the world is against us. Our minds assume that there is something wrong with us and that everyone hates us for it. But that's usually not the case.

#MobMentality

#MobMentality is when you are bullied publicly on social media and suddenly people from everywhere (who know you and who don't know you) join in on the bullying. Why? Well, kids who bully believe they are invincible behind their computers. I was cyberstalked and cyberbullied many times, and I later discovered that half of the people who were bullying me had never even met me. I hadn't even heard their names before. How crazy is that?

#Anonymous

The most painful part of it all was not that people were writing me cruel messages, but that I had no idea who these people were. They could be the people who were nice to me, they could be the people I looked up to, they could be anyone. And when it comes to cyberbullying, anyone can target you for anything.

The fact that the person bullying can be anonymous tears apart your personal life. Every relationship, friendship, or connection you have is clouded with skepticism: "Are they my cyberbully?"

#CYBERHAUNTING

When we are cyberbullied, our mind wanders from person to person in our life and assumes that almost everyone in our life is bullying us online. It's that constant mystery as to who this person is and why he or she would do such a thing. And there is no escape. **With cell phones, computers, and apps, cyberbullying can haunt you every second of every day. And if you are being cyberbullied and don't do anything to prevent it, then you become a bystander to your own bullying situation.**

When I went through cyberbullying, I had to change my phone number, block lots of people on social media, and essentially restart my #CyberLife. If you lose yourself in social media, you may also lose part of yourself in the real world. You might be so obsessed with what people say to you and who you are online that you forget about living life in the real world and loving yourself. Eventually, social media will become more important than who you are and it will consume your life. We need to end this haunting.

#CYBERWEAPON

Cyberbullying is a Digital Weapon of Total Destruction (#DWOTD).

Here's a list of the ammunition used by the cyberbully:

#24/7

#anonymous

#voiceless

#faceless

#contagious (as in viral; new people might jump into the fight and add fuel to the fire)

#difficult2delete

#feared and/or #ignored by schools and teachers

#hidden from parents and teachers

The truth of the matter is this: Cyberbullies are sometimes considered criminals and can be convicted of a crime. You need to save yourself. DO NOT stay silent. You need to take action.

#GOINGDARK

Want to stop or avoid being cyberbullied? One option: **GO DARK!** Take a break from social media and delete your Facebook page, delete your Twitter account, delete your accounts on websites where people have anonymous accounts, delete everything that you know may lead to a bad situation.

Don't expect it to be easy. You may go through a period of withdrawal where all you want to do is be on social media and it almost pains you not to be. You can ease your way into it if you like. You can go partially dark by deleting or disabling some of your social media. Then you can slowly delete or disable the rest. It doesn't have to be permanent either. Look at it as if you are taking a vacation from it all. It will always be there to go back to.

You can be bullied on any website. That's the danger of the cyberworld. I was constantly cyberbullied on Facebook, instant message, text message, everything. I even received voice mails and calls from people using disguised voices. I guess my classmates were trying to make me feel like everyone was against me, even people I didn't know. Or maybe they thought they were being funny. I don't know. But it was terrifying and very confusing.

That being said, deleting social media doesn't mean you won't be cyberattacked. People still may make jokes or post things that are terrible, but at least you won't be seeing them. You also won't be able to be reached if you go dark.

#GOING(ALMOST)DARK

It's natural to want to feel connected, and social media helps with that. But you must protect your own well-being. You can go "almost dark." Choose one or two social media sites to be on. That way there are fewer venues on which to be targeted. **Be sure to understand and use the privacy settings on each site to protect yourself.** Also, you can consider having a profile that is anonymous so you cannot be easily reached.

#CYBERPOSSIBILITIES

Let's not forget that the Internet has lots of positive possibilities, too. You can read blogs and group posts that are related to your interests, feelings, and situation. You can watch videos and vlogs that brighten your day! You can also venture into becoming a blogger or YouTuber yourself. The possibilities are endless! There are also forums and groups you can be a part of, but it's important to be careful when talking to people online—especially ones you don't know. Never agree to meet someone you don't know in person. Don't give out personal information either. If you use the Internet wisely, it can be a great resource for you.

#PRIVACY

If you choose not to go dark, you need to know the privacy settings like the back of your hand, and use them on all of the sites you use. You aren't weird for doing this. In fact, celebrities and people in the spotlight have to do the same thing. They receive a lot of love, but they also receive a tremendous amount of hate. You are not alone.

#CYBERLANGUAGE

Bullies may change their typing patterns and cyberlanguage with each message to appear as a different person. This makes us think that there are a lot of people bullying us. But it really could be just one or two people. They are afraid and hiding behind their computer, perhaps the most cowardly act of all.

#CYBERBIZ

These social media websites and apps are businesses—they may not protect you. Once again, you must protect yourself.

Cyberbullies are not invincible. In order to protect your own well-being, you must print out or take pictures of all of the evidence of cyberbullying. You must report this information to your parents or a teacher so they can help you figure out how to deal with this. When your life and well-being are at stake, you never, ever wait.

In cyberspace, information is a lethal weapon. Don't tell anyone anything that you want to keep private. The currency of bullying is information. If your secret comes back to you it is because you told someone. Your privacy is your responsibility. At the end of the day, you must customize your online experience so you feel safe and comfortable. Be your own superhero.

SURVIVAL TIP

Owning the Problem

You cannot expect social media companies to own the bullying problem. You should absolutely report the problem to web or app administrators, but that doesn't mean it will solve anything other than maybe getting the post or comment removed.

CHECK YOUR #DAMAGE

You've read the entire chapter. You know the effects of cyberbullying. You know how it can affect you. And you probably have an idea of where you are in the cycle. You need to check your damage. How much have you suffered? How much have you accepted? I don't know what you have been through. Only you know that. You need to check in with yourself.

The Cyberbullying Damage Chart below gives you a 1–6 scale for measuring your pain. Hopefully, it will help you see where you are.

CYBERBULLYING DAMAGE CHART

Check a Box

1 ☐ I'm not cyberbullied at all. I have no problems on social media.

2 ☐ I'm cyberbullied infrequently. It hasn't started to bother me. It's just some drama. I don't feel that I need to do anything about it.

3 ☐ I'm cyberbullied sometimes. It makes me feel uncomfortable and nervous, but I'm not scared. Though I'm worried that it will get worse.

4 ☐ I'm cyberbullied often but it's not every day. I'm feeling a little haunted by it. I feel depressed and I'm scared when it happens.

5 ☐ I'm cyberbullied every day. When I'm not on the Internet, it's hard to get through the day because I feel sick and scared. It makes me feel so bad about myself. I don't know what to do.

6 ☐ I'm cyberbullied all of the time. I'm totally haunted by it. I can't escape. I feel that someone wants to hurt me. I don't know how to get help. I'm so scared and my life is a total wreck.

If you are in the position of 4-6 you need to go dark or consider another solution to fix your situation ASAP. You need to protect yourself. Do not stay silent. Reach out to your parents or another adult. You can also block people who are bullying you and report it to the administrators of the website or app. **If you are in the position of 2 or 3,** I would suggest going almost dark or just altering your privacy settings. You are important. You need to protect yourself.

Social media is wonderful in terms of communication, creativity, information, and entertainment. At the same time, when you post your private life on the Internet or talk to people you don't know or trust, you are putting yourself out there in a very vulnerable way. You have the right to do and say anything you want. You do not deserve to be bullied. But know that other kids might not like what you're saying and bully you. This is why discovering the Real You is so important. The great thing about the Real You is that you get to define what you think is cool or not cool. Remember: You are always changing. Therefore, what you think is cool will always change. But being safe on the Internet is always important. You are your own number one priority.

Dedicated to my love of acting

Unmasked

"Why do you love it?" he asked
And I whispered "Have you ever lived
    without a mask?
Or wondered what it's like to travel down
    someone else's path?"

There are worlds beyond
Untouched and un dawned
Waiting for us to come along
And tell their un tolds
Of those who have passed
Alone and in the cold
With stories richer than the finest of golds

Or you may find a moment
Where you are chained to the darkest
    corners of your brain
And you loathe the confines of your very name
I love it then more than anything else
It may seem absurd
But in that time
I am able to blur
The line

Between reality
And all that is unseen and unheard
I can become a peasant who dreams
   of wealth
Or a queen who despises every bit of herself

I lose my name
And allow my soul
To take control
Time desists
And all that exists
Is
Essence

I live to act
But in truth
I am much more than that
I am the explorer
The excavator
And the messenger
To all that lies
Buried and un intact
And so I responded to his question
"I love it because I can live many lives
   unknown and unmasked."

CHAPTER EIGHT

Creativity:
Being Happy Again

Ever since I was a little girl, I was always a creative person. I would make up stories and play by myself for hours. I would write constantly and draw all over the place. But as soon as I started getting bullied, it seemed like my creativity just disappeared. I couldn't figure out where it went or why it left me. And I felt like I needed it more than ever. So for years I didn't write, I didn't act, I didn't really do anything creative.

I was frozen. And it was horrible.

But in 6th grade, I couldn't take it anymore. I needed an outlet. So I started acting in the school plays. At first I wasn't very good. Acting is most successful when you can tap into your own feelings. But my emotions were still hidden deep within me. **I tried not to feel, because if I did, then I would feel EVERYTHING.** I guess I was afraid it would be too overwhelming. But as I got more confidence in my creativity and more belief in myself, I released my feelings into my art. It was incredible! Suddenly I was good at something, but more important, I felt happiest doing it.

Creativity is one of the remarkable parts of being human. In one way or another, we all have creativity. Whether we are born with it or we develop it throughout our lives, we can be creative in all forms. Scientists, doctors, teachers, YouTubers, bloggers, painters, writers, dancers, athletes, construction workers, lawyers, chefs— these people are all creative in one way or another.

So you may be wondering, what is a creative person?

Cre•a•tive: having or showing an ability to make new things or think of new ideas

SURVIVAL TIP

Hiding emotions deep within yourself is overwhelming for the body and mind. It's not healthy. While it may not be possible to let out all of your emotions while being bullied, you must understand that there is a time for everything and eventually you will be comfortable with the idea of expressing all your emotions.

HOW DID I REDISCOVER MY CREATIVITY?

When I was 14, I moved with my family to California. At that point, I could feel my desire to be creative bubbling up inside of me. Maybe you feel the same thing I did. I felt like . . .

✳ I had to do something really important but I didn't know how or what it was.

✳ I had this burning, nauseous feeling in the pit of my stomach.

✳ I was anxious and jittery.

So I started to pay close attention to the world around me. I figured that if there was something I had to do, it would show up in a sign somewhere in my life. I waited for a year. Nothing happened.

Then one day it all changed. I was on my way to class and decided to take a different path. I walked into the senior quad (which I usually would never do because I was intimidated by the seniors). Right before entering the quad, I saw a poster for a film festival. It was advertising a screenwriting and filmmaking competition for students. It was the day of the deadline for all scripts.

I had never written a screenplay before, but I knew I had to do it. This poster was the sign I had been waiting for. It was a sign that my creativity would come back to me. It was a sign that I needed to have tremendous bravery to embark on this path. It was a sign that I was ready. And I was not afraid. I didn't think about it—I JUST DID IT!

I went home and stayed up really late and wrote my very first script and submitted it that night. I wrote about bullying. It poured out of me. I had so much to say about what bullying does to kids. I talked about what it felt like to be bullied and how it affects kids even years after it stops. I wound up winning the screenwriting competition and having my short film made. And from that moment on, I made a promise to myself. I would not let my gifts for writing and acting go to waste.

Being creative might change how people look at you. But if this gets you closer to the Real You, then it's a sacrifice worth making.

SURVIVAL TIP

Don't be afraid of what people might think of you and your creativity.

It's your life—not anyone else's. And if you let your peers influence your creativity, then you aren't living your life. This is really hard to do because we all want to fit in. Believe me, I know because I'm still working on doing what I'm telling you to do.

HOW DO YOU FIND YOUR CREATIVITY?

You might already be aware of your creativity but not quite sure what to do with it. This is very normal. You also might have no idea that you are creative. Again, this is very normal. I can promise that you have the potential to be creative, and we are going to figure out where.

Let's begin with school. I believe that interest in certain subjects is a good sign of creativity. Which classes do you find interesting? **English, Math, Science, History, Foreign Language, Art, Theater, Music (instrument or voice), Sports.**

If absolutely none of these subjects are interesting to you, it's not a problem. Your creativity is just somewhere else! There are plenty of things you can do to find that niche.

What can you do to find your creativity in the area that you are interested in?

Disconnect. Spend time alone without the distraction of computers, TV, cell phones, video games, and even music. You need to let your brain relax and have time to think without stimulation. Set aside at least a half hour for this every day. Take care of your brain and your brain will take care of your creativity. This can be done indoors and outdoors—it's totally up to you and you can alternate from day to day.

Sleep. If you don't sleep eight or nine hours a night, you won't be able to think at your best. Do not stay up late on your computer or phone, because that will stimulate your brain and make it harder to fall asleep. It's hard to be creative when you're exhausted or amped up.

Read about what's going on in the world. It always gives me ideas. Whether you read the newspaper or find a news site online, your creativity will take inspiration from what is going on in the world.

Expose yourself to what's offered around you. Whether it's a lecture, museum exhibit, play, anything, check it out. Even if you don't think you'll like it, you never know who you will meet, what you will learn, or what tiny thing will inspire you.

Watch films. Select those that are well done and classic. You may hate some and you may love some. Check out the American Film Institute's 100 greatest American films.

If you enjoy something, immerse yourself in it. It could be math, bird-watching, reading about the moon, jet planes, growing tomatoes, or debate club. If you really do enjoy it, that's a good sign. Don't let the opportunity go to waste.

Talk to people who seem creative. Tell them about yourself, what you like, what you want to learn or accomplish. Have discussions with interesting people and see where that leads you.

Listen to music that you like. It's easy to just listen to the hottest songs on the iTunes Top 100. Then you'll be like everyone else and fit in, right? But why would you want to be like everyone else? Try to find some music that you like, even if it isn't popular.

Exercise. You need to release your stress to be more creative.

Love yourself. It's hard to love every part of yourself, but try to find a part of yourself that you do love. And tell that part that you love it. And thank it for being a part of you. Because you should love every part of yourself. Treat yourself right and creativity will come to you.

The more in touch you are with yourself, the more creative you will be.

Remember: You have this creativity within you and it's only a matter of time before it reveals itself. It may take longer than you think or hope, so be patient. But every little thing you create will help reveal your gifts to you. Think of it as a caterpillar trying to turn into a butterfly.

OWNING YOUR CREATIVITY

Once you have discovered and acknowledged your creativity, see where it leads you. It may change your style, the way you speak, your attitude, and more. Creativity is a powerful thing that has a personality of its own. So let your creativity flow into the Real You. If you are connected to your creativity, it may even start changing your life. It may attract new friends (who are more like you), new opportunities (which you may have always wanted), or just a new sense of self.

Being confident in your own skin will make you a happier person, even when it's hard and you feel like you aren't accepted. It will feel better to be WHO YOU REALLY ARE. I can say this because I know what it is like to pretend to be someone else just to be liked, and I also know what it is like to be myself. Don't get me wrong, it's not always easy to be who you really are. It's not always comfortable or "safe." But when it's good, it's really good.

SURVIVAL TIP

You don't have to pretend to be cool or confident. When you are your creative self, there is no pretending. It's one of the nicest feelings that you will ever know.

My New Beginning

I suddenly feel so free
And I wonder if it's just a dream
I wonder when I'm going to wake up
   and scream
Or maybe I won't this time
Maybe bullying is no longer a theme
In my life
Maybe I've felt enough pain
Maybe I have enough strength
And so I look back at my life
And I see an abandoned path I now leave
It's scary to me
As much pain as it caused
It's still a part of me

But then I look ahead
And I see the most beautiful path
Shining so bright
I know it's my human right to enter that path
To not feel sad
Or bad
That I'm starting over
That I'm about to enter
My new beginning

free
free

And so I put one foot in front of the other
Take it step by step
Count my breaths
And I near that path

As I'm about to cross over
I hear something say
"Don't be afraid. Everything is going to be okay."
And I realize that's true
I no longer need to suffer through my days
Or make do
Just because that is the only option I have
I know what it's like to fall
And I know what it's like to fly

So leap forward onto that path
I have made my choice
I am going to fly

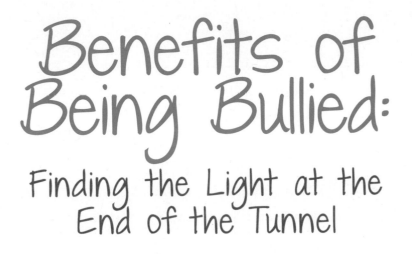

CHAPTER NINE

Benefits of Being Bullied:

Finding the Light at the End of the Tunnel

I remember my 8th grade graduation. As it ended, I sat on a bench thinking about my five years at that school. I knew I was leaving the school and moving to California. A part of me felt free for the first time in five years. I would be away from all of the people who caused me so much pain. But another part of me felt anchored, like I would always be partially stuck at that school—in the hallways, in the classrooms, and in every place where I was bullied. I was so frustrated by this. And that is when I said out loud (when no one was around), **"What was all of this for?"**

And at the exact moment that those words left my mouth, there was an incredible gust of wind. And I could swear that I heard these next words in that wind: **"Something bigger than you."**

The biggest benefit of my experience with bullying is this book. I felt like I had to write this book because I was lucky enough to make it through so many years of torment. I was lucky enough to get to move to California and find my passion in life. I could not turn to the next chapter in my life until I used my experience to help you and every other kid who knows what it is like to feel worthless. That day, on that bench, I made a promise to myself that I would do "something bigger."

Me and You

You might be thinking, "What good could possibly come from being bullied?"

And to be honest with you, until a few years ago, I wasn't sure that anything good could come from being bullied. But I've realized that it can be one of the biggest gifts.

This book is for you . . . but it's also for me. This book has been my healing. It has helped me let go of a part of my history and get ready to begin a new chapter.

It's not easy to start a new chapter of a book when you're used to the page you're on. It might not be a very good page, but it's familiar and comfortable. But familiar and comfortable is not the way to live. And if you stay on that one page, then you'll never know what will happen in the next chapter. Trying new things can be scary. After all, who knows what might lie ahead. But it's worth taking the risk and trying.

This book was created to show you that you CAN GET THROUGH THIS. When I wrote it, I wanted you to know that no matter how many people put you down, no matter how many people leave you feeling broken, and no matter how alone you feel in this world—I BELIEVE IN YOU.

So another benefit to being bullied is the understanding that when you are loved and supported, you can change your life forever!

Other Benefits from Being Bullied

I cannot promise that everyone reading this book will have exactly the same benefits. I can promise you, however, if you take this journey you are opening yourself up to the possibility of changing your life for the better. My life has completely changed throughout this journey. And I am grateful for my experiences both good and bad. Why? Because I know:

I am strong. I know how strong I am and that I can get through very tough times.

I am determined. I have goals and I will achieve them, no matter who tries to stand in my way. This is partially due to the fact that for all of the years I was bullied, I was told I was worthless, useless, and stupid by my peers. So that has been part of the fuel for my fire.

I am a hard worker. This is also partially due to how kids treated me. I know that in order to achieve my goals, I must work very hard. I know what it's like to feel worthless and I am not interested in feeling that way ever again. So I will work hard to achieve my dreams.

I am comfortable in my own skin. I'm not afraid to make jokes, to be silly, or to be different anymore. I lived so much of my life trying to be a certain way because I thought that was how to fit in and be loved. But it's not. And I am so much happier now.

I am smart. I can understand people and social situations fast. I think this is partially because when I was bullied I had to learn to adapt quickly.

I am grateful. Because I lived so many years in an unhealthy environment, I am now so grateful for where I am in my life and the people around me. I think I appreciate it so much more because I have experienced bullying. So when I meet a really kind, good person, I know that he or she is to be treasured.

I am connected to myself. I have been able to know myself. I have been able to love myself. I have become my own best friend. When you are alone and isolated for so many years, you are faced with who you truly are.

I am something bigger. When I moved to California, I needed to find a purpose. And that's when I found my love for writing, acting, and film. I have not only discovered that I am good at something, but that I have a reason to do it. I am here for "something bigger." I am here to "give a voice to the voiceless" and to do my part in changing the world.

I am undefined. I am not defined by bullying. I am not defined by my past. I am not a victim. I am not a bullied girl. I am undefined, just like you can be undefined. We can choose how we want to be defined, but I do not want to be defined by anything. I came into this world as a soul in a body. And I will not let anyone or any action alter who I came into this world to be. So I ask you—what extraordinary things can come from your journey of overcoming bullying? What are your benefits? What do you want to do in this life? Who do you want to be?

Bullying does not define you. Nothing does. You have every possibility in this world.

I wanted to help you through the jungle. I wanted you to know that you can get through this and truly thrive. You may face more roadblocks or bumps, but you now know that you can get past it. You are the Real You. Do not let anything hold you back. Embrace your new life and be who you want to be on this miraculous planet.

Ready, set, go.

✦ EPILOGUE ✦

I WAS FINALLY FREE of my
bullies when my family and I moved across the country
at the end of 8th grade. But I wasn't free of the heavy
feelings about my experiences. **I felt sick, guilty, and
lost.** I couldn't figure out why. And then one day I
understood. I had escaped my bullying situation, but
there were millions of kids around the world who were
being bullied every single day. If I didn't do something
about it, then I was no different from a bystander or a
hypocrite.

I was so desperate to help other kids out there and
write this book that I didn't think about how I would be
exposing my heart and my history to the world. I didn't
think about how I could possibly be bullied again for
publishing my book.

On the morning of October 1, 2014, my ebook was
released. Suddenly, I was enveloped in nerves. What if
my past came back to haunt me? What if I was bullied
again? What if I had never really escaped it all?

Two days later, every worry in my mind disappeared.
I had my first speaking engagement at a school. I was
going to give a talk about bullying to 150 4th, 5th, and
6th graders. What happened on that day was far beyond
anything that I could have ever imagined.

When I was done with my speech, so many of the kids gathered around me. They even skipped their recess to talk to me! They told me how they were being bullied. They asked for my advice. They told me how important my book was. And they said that I was their inspiration.

I saw myself in every one of those kids. I saw the fear, desperation, confusion, sadness—I saw it all as if I was one of them. And then it all made sense, I AM one of them. Even though I was 19 years old, the torment I endured in school would always be a part of me. I don't live with it every day anymore, but that doesn't mean that it doesn't live within me.

After that day, I realized that whatever negativity I was to receive from my book didn't matter. If I could help kids everywhere with my book, then that was all that mattered. Because I had gotten through my tough times. But those kids were still going through it—alone and lost. No matter how much hate I could possibly receive, I was still free from my bullies. But millions of kids weren't.

As the days went by after my book was released, I braced myself for the hate. But instead I received a flood of love. **I received messages from ALL OVER THE WORLD.** Kids in elementary school, middle school, and high school wrote to me about how my book changed their lives and that I was their inspiration. Parents and teachers told me about how my book helped their daughter, son, student, or friend. Even adults wrote to me to say that my book healed their bullying scars from years ago!

And in that moment, I realized that everything happens for a reason. It might take years and years to figure out why something bad happens, but there is always good in the bad. All along, there was a reason that I was bullied. I was meant to write this book. I was meant to show you and every other kid who is being bullied that YOU CAN—AND WILL—GET THROUGH THIS.

And in those moments when you feel that there is no hope, remember that I have had those moments, too. And so has every other person who has been bullied. But we must keep going. We must do everything we can to heal ourselves and make our situations better because we are all destined to be something great.

✦ Q&A WITH AIJA ✦

Q: If you could go back in time, what advice would you give yourself?

A: I'd tell young Aija so many things. But first, I would give her a BIG hug. I would then tell her that even though she may not believe it, everything will get so much better.

Then, I would say the following:

✦ Do your best to communicate with your parents, Aija. Tell them everything, even if it seems silly to you. Tell them how you feel. Don't be ashamed of what you are going through. They can help you more than anyone else.

✦ No matter what anyone says to you, Aija, don't let it destroy how you feel about yourself. You are not fat. You are not ugly. You are not stupid. You are a beautiful, intelligent, and very special girl who is destined for great things.

✦ Don't just accept the bullying. I know it's scary to speak up, but you should try it. There are so many things you can do to try and make the situation better.

* Never, ever lose sight of the light at the end of the tunnel. I PROMISE you that things will get so much better. You have no idea how incredible your life will be in just a few years. You have no idea how happy you will be and how many friends you will have. I know you don't believe it, but let the idea of it power you through. It will get better. Just you wait and see. In the meantime, keep trying to improve your life, even if it's in small ways. Try to make friends in other social circles; join clubs, teams, or after-school activities. Also, communicate with your trusted loved ones about what you're going through.

Q: How are you able to give such good advice about bullying?

A: I've gathered my tips in a variety of ways:

* **Personal experience.** Once I started writing this book, I was able to put my thoughts and feelings about all my experiences with bullying into words. Suddenly, I found myself thinking of all of these tips and tricks that I wished I had when I was younger. But I couldn't have had the perspective to write these tips without enduring bullying for so many years.

* **My parents.** My parents are incredibly supportive and understanding. Since they have more life experience than I do, their advice, opinions, and tips were really valuable.

* **Professionals.** I talked to teachers, psychologists, and doctors about this book. Often, their knowledge and advice was so different from anything I came up with or my parents shared with me. I had long conversations with doctors, including Myrna Fleishman, PhD, a very experienced therapist. We talked about the best tactics for overcoming bullying. Additionally, one of my teachers changed my life with one simple sentence: "It is never your fault that you are being bullied." Every source of information is unique and when you pair the advice of professionals with the advice of your parents or loved one, it's a jackpot.

Q: How do you get up after being knocked down so many times?

A: A boxer doesn't give up when he or she loses a match. He gets back in the ring. He could quit, but he doesn't. He knows he has a chance at winning, so he tries again. That's what you have to do. Try again.

There were times where I was so sick of *trying again*—trying to make friends, trying to be happy, trying to focus on school. I just wanted to escape. But every time I was knocked down, I made the decision to get back up. It might have taken me 10 minutes or 10 hours to get back in the game, but I did. I got back up because I had dreams. I got back up because I wanted a bright future. I got back up because I had to believe in myself. I brushed off the dirt, held my head high, and took it moment by moment.

Through all my experience, I learned something pretty incredible that helped me get through the tough times: You must decide to get back up, even before you get knocked down.

Q: How did you learn to trust again?

A: After my experiences with bullying, I often questioned people and their motives. But eventually, I realized that if I didn't trust myself to choose friends, then how would I ever find friends? I also realized that in life, you win some and you lose some. But you have to keep trying.

So I started to trust myself and my instincts. If I didn't have a good gut feeling about someone, I would remember that. It didn't mean that I couldn't be friendly with that person, but it did mean that I needed to stay alert.

Trusting myself and my gut feelings has led me to some incredible friendships. I've met people who

I love and laugh with. I've also had disappointments. But I wouldn't be able to tell a good friend from a bad friend if I hadn't had those disappointments.

Q: What do I do if a teacher is bullying me?

A: Teachers are supposed to be there to support you. But in some cases, teachers can be the bully. I've been in this situation myself. I know how scary and confusing it can be. Who do you turn to in this case? Who can you possibly trust? I told my parents what was going on, and they did their best to try and help, but nothing changed. At least they knew why I got a bad grade on a test or wanted to skip class. Most importantly, I knew my parents were by my side.

It's important to understand the difference between a teacher who is a bully and one who is strict or mean. A bullying teacher uses his or her power to punish, embarrass, or put down a student beyond reasonable disciplinary procedures. If you think a teacher is bullying you, talk to your parents about this issue since it can be especially hard to understand. You can also look at the list in the beginning of the book about what bullying is.

There are many ways to help the situation.

★ You parents can arrange a meeting with your teacher to calmly talk about the issue.

* You should document the bullying. Write down the events that took place, including dates, times, and specific details. If you have meetings with your parents or your teacher, document those, too. This is all very important!

* You can talk to your advisor, another teacher, or school counselor or nurse. Tell them about your situation and ask for their advice.

* If talking directly with your teacher doesn't help, you and your parents can talk to the principal, superintendent, or school board. If you are being bullied by this teacher, other kids might be, too.

Q: How do you forgive/should I forgive?

A: Forgiveness is something that cannot be forced. And you don't HAVE TO forgive to let go of your past. It's all personal and unique to you. But I found it very helpful.

One day, not that long ago, I was able to forgive one of the kids who bullied me. I can honestly say that I didn't expect to ever be ready to forgive. I was holding on so tightly—so afraid to let go. But when I was face-to-face with the kid who bullied me, something changed. I felt no fear, sadness, anger, or frustration. I felt nothing. It was the most beautiful feeling. And actually, this one act of forgiveness turned out to be symbolic of me forgiving my entire experience with bullying.

I didn't actually say to this kid, "I forgive you." I told myself. The forgiveness was for me. It was time to let go. That doesn't mean that he and I will ever be friends. That doesn't mean that I will say hi to him if I see him again. Even though I have forgiven him, I don't want to include him in my life.

When you are ready to forgive, you will know. It could take 3 days, 5 months, or 10 years. Or you may never be ready to forgive. And that's all okay, too. You must do what is best for you. No one can judge you on this matter. But if one day you are ready to forgive, you will know the feeling that I have described.

Q: What do you do if no one listens to you?

A: Never ever give up trying. There is someone out there who will listen to you and who will help you. And sometimes you have to meet the wrong people in order to find the right people.

No matter how many disappointments you have, you must keep trying. You will feel like you are invisible. You will feel like your voice is the wind, but that should only give you more strength and more power.

For years, I thought that I would never meet teachers, kids, or other adults who would actually listen. I figured that if I had met a hundred who didn't listen, that meant that the rest were all the same. But I was so wrong. I did finally find a teacher who helped me. And I did meet real friends—ones who not only listened to me but also heard me.

I know it seems impossible now, but I'll be the first person to tell you that the word "impossible" means nothing. It's only impossible if you say it's impossible. I know it can happen for you just as it happened for me.

✱ HOTLINES ✱

Boys Town National Hotline:
1-800-448-3000 or
www.boystown.org/hotline
  • Free
  • 24/7, 365 days a year
  • Staffed with trained counselors
  • Has a Spanish-speaking line
  • Has online chat and texting
    services

GLBT National Helpline for Youth:
1-800-246-7743 or
www.glnh.org/talkline
  • Free
  • Confidential
  • Available M–F from 1 PM–9 PM
    (PST) and Saturday 9 AM–2 PM
    (PST)
  • Has an online chat and e-mail
    support

**National Suicide Prevention
Hotline:**
1-800-273-8255 or
www.suicidepreventionlifeline.org
  • Free
  • 24/7, 365 days a year
  • Confidential
  • Has a Spanish-speaking line

Stomp Out Bullying:
Online Chat:
www.stompoutbullying.org
  • Free
  • Confidential
  • Staffed with trained volunteers

Teen Line:
www.teenlineonline.org or
310-855-4673 or 800-852-8336
  • Speak to other teens about what
    you're feeling
  • Toll free in California only
  • Available from 6 PM–10 PM (PST)
    every night
  • Text "TEEN" to 839863 between
    5:30 PM and 9:30 PM (PST) to
    talk to teens—standard texting
    rates may apply
  • Message boards are always
    available on their website

Trevor Lifeline:
866-488-7386
  • Free
  • Available 24/7
  • Staffed with trained volunteer
    counselors
  • TrevorChat, TrevorText,
    TrevorSpace, AskTrevor all
    available through
    *www.thetrevorproject.org/pages/
    get help now*

✶ ACKNOWLEDGMENTS ✶

There are so many people I want to thank for their support and involvement in this book. Without their belief in me, it would not be in your hands today.

It is a dream come true to be a Scholastic author. I feel enormously privileged to be working with the incredible Scholastic team. Thank you for embracing me and this book. Debra Dorfman and Samantha Schutz truly understand kids and teens and their contribution to *The Survival Guide to Bullying* has been remarkable. I'd also like to thank Liz Herzog and Maya Frank-Levine for their hard work on design and production.

Thank you Deborah Temkin, PhD, for reviewing this book so closely and making sure that it would be as helpful to as many kids as possible.

This book started as a self-published ebook. I was so fortunate to work with Michael Harkavy, the editorial consultant on this project. Thank you, Michael, for your guidance, brilliance, sensitivity, and support. You inspired me every day!

Myrna Fleishman, PhD, is an experienced therapist in Santa Barbara, California. Myrna and I had many conversations about the different faces of bullying. Her expertise and depth were so important to my writing. Thank you, Myrna.

It was my dream to work on the original ebook design with Karen Hsu, Alice Chung, and Julie Cho at Omnivore. Thank you for making the ebook so beautiful and for embracing this project.

The Santa Barbara International Film Festival changed my life. Thank you for giving me the opportunity to discover my passions and trusting me with life-changing opportunities.

Thank you to my literary agent and attorney, Jay Kramer, for helping to bring this book to life.

There are so many people who have both inspired me and believed in me over the years. Thank you Gay Abel-Bey, Michael Goi, Denise Albert, Sam Zises and Learned Media, Paula Allen, and Rowland Holmes.

To my brother, Max: You are my best friend. You always understand me and bring your wisdom and humor to my life every day. Thank you for being the best brother and friend I could ever ask for.

To Elliot Mayrock, my dad: Your incredibly wise, loving, and understanding nature guides and teaches me every day. You are the most remarkable father and human being. Thank you for allowing me to pursue my wildest dreams. Thank you for loving me always.

To Alecia Mayrock, my mom: Your belief, support, and endless love for me have given me the strength that I need to pursue my dreams. Your enormous generosity and dedication are what have allowed this project to come to life. I am the luckiest daughter to have you as a mother and best friend. Thank you for believing in my vision and for loving me always.

To all of the people who ever put me down to the point where I didn't know if I had any more strength:

Thank you for showing me just how strong I am.

✷ ABOUT THE AUTHOR ✷

Aija Mayrock started writing this book when she was sixteen years old and finished it in 2015, at nineteen years old. She promised herself that she would publish this book as her gift to the next generation of kids who will be bullied. Aija dealt with bullying for many years, beginning in the 3rd grade. In the midst of these very difficult times, Aija discovered her creativity and passion. She wrote her very first screenplay on the day of the deadline for the Santa Barbara International Film Festival 10-10-10 competition. She won the competition and from that time forth pursued her passions. Since then, Aija has continued to work with the Santa Barbara International Film Festival. She has also won awards from the Scholastic Art and Writing Competition for her writing and poetry.

Aija is a writer, actress, and filmmaker. Her dream is to give a voice to the voiceless through art.

For more information, and to hear Aija recite one of her "roems," visit www.aijamayrock.com.